Playing IN
THE **PUDDLES**

This is an IndieMosh book

brought to you by MoshPit Publishing
an imprint of Mosher's Business Support Pty Ltd

PO BOX 147
Hazelbrook NSW 2779

www.indiemosh.com.au

First published 2015 © Barnaby Howarth

Cataloguing-in-Publication entry is available from the National Library of Australia: http://catalogue.nla.gov.au/

Title:	Playing in the Puddles
Author:	Howarth, Barnaby
ISBN:	978-1-925219-81-4 (paperback)
	978-1-925219-82-1 (ebook – epub)
	978-1-925219-83-8 (ebook – mobi)

Cover picture courtesy of Luke Turner Photography

Cover design by Danny Ryan, Creative Director/Designer @ echelonDMR

Playing IN
THE PUDDLES

Barnaby Howarth

Barnaby would like to thank everybody ...

Contents

Foreword by Luke

(the man who got involved in the fight that resulted in Barnaby having a stroke)

The night I found out Barnaby had suffered a stroke I knew my tears were pointless. I knew they would fix nothing, but they wouldn't stop. A week earlier I had seen him lie motionless on the pavement. Briefly, I thought he was dead.

While I didn't start the fight, I could have walked away. I should have walked away.

He remained in a coma as the rest of the Pennant Hills Demons AFL team took the field two days after his stroke. Our team had been impossible to beat all season but on this day we were trounced. As is Barns' respect in the competition, the opposition's guilt was palpable as they kicked goal after goal against us.

I owed Barns a debt I could never repay, and I played my heart out as he, the heart of our team, lay motionless in a hospital bed several kilometres away.

The first time I saw him in hospital after he regained consciousness was devastating. I could tell his mental spark, his humour and his wit remained, but they were trapped inside a body that could no longer keep up.

Almost ten years on and Barns is still physically afflicted as a result of that night. Despite this he has told me he sometimes thinks that out of the two of us, it is he who got off easy. Not a week goes by where I don't think about Barnaby and how my actions affected him and his entire world. I contend Barnes can only suggest he got off easy as he has made his recovery look easy. He has leapt every hurdle and conquered every barrier placed in front of him. One step at a time he took on small tasks and once those were completed, he set himself to accomplish big challenges.

Such a selfless character, he doesn't just strive to better himself, he strives to show others they can do the same. This is the fuel that fires him. A leader of humans, Barnaby Howarth picks you up and then carries you along with him. He has never tired of this, no matter how many hardships he has faced.

This biography spells that out.

Up until we started corresponding to produce this foreword, I felt our friendship could never be the same. Even though Barns has honestly stated he holds me no ill will, my guilt could never be buried deep enough and I could never be sorry enough to him, his family and friends. The hideous scar our relationship bares upsets and shames me whenever I look back upon it. Since reading this biography and speaking to Barns however, he has given me the gift of being able to look forward. Possibly the last person in the world he should uplift he has.

Luke

Introduction

Thursday June 18th 2005

'Fancy going on to a club?' said Luke as the four friends piled out of the pub. 'Not for us, mate,' said Patty, meaning him and Johnny. 'Work tomorrow; we'd better get back to the hotel.'

'Anybody hungry?' said Barnaby. 'We could grab a pie at the 7-11.'

'Yeah, why not?' said Patty and they headed off down the road.

Luke saw a group of guys hanging about outside the store and his heart sank. They had 'trouble' written all over them. Sure enough, as they got closer the three men stirred into action and started to act tough.

One of the gang shouldered Barnaby as he walked up to the door. 'Woah, sorry mate,' Barnaby said as Luke got the same treatment. 'Look, we don't want any trouble, alright? We're not interested in a fight.'

The men said nothing, but they barged into Barnaby and Luke again as if to assert their dominance.

As the friends went in and got their food, Luke wondered if they were wrong to always back away from trouble. They never went looking for it, but being young and male, trouble sometimes went out of its way to find them, especially when it was in the form of idiots like the three outside the 7-11 that night.

When the friends came back out, the gang of three were giving somebody else a hard time; they sat down on a bench and ate their food.

'Right, it's definitely time for us to head off now,' said Johnny as he finished eating. 'Great night, guys. Catch you later!'

'Okay, guys,' said Barnaby. 'Later!'

'I fancy a pineapple doughnut,' said Luke. 'Get you one?'

'No thanks,' said Barnaby.

Patty and Johnny walked off down the road to get to their hotel and Luke headed back towards the store. As he neared the 7-11 the three came at him again, this time with another bloke behind them yelling all kinds of abuse. Two of them got right in his face, but Luke wasn't rising to the bait.

'I'm not going to fight you, guys. I don't want any trouble, okay?' he said as he pushed the door open and went into the shop.

While he was being served, Luke was thinking about the guys outside. It was clear they weren't going to rest until they fought someone, and they'd probably beat them up pretty badly. What if some young kid came by and they started in on him? He wouldn't stand a chance against those Neanderthals. As he pocketed his change and picked up his doughnut, he came to a decision: he was big and could handle himself; if anyone was going to give them a scrap, it should be him, rather than the next kid who walked in after the bars shut. With a bit of luck once they'd had their fun they'd leave.

Afterwards Luke admitted that he might not have been thinking straight, but at the time it all made perfect sense.

Sure enough, as he left the 7-11 the pushing and name calling started again. 'Here, mate, catch!' he said as he threw the doughnut to Barnaby. 'Don't jump in, I know what I'm doing.' He turned to the aggressors. 'OK, lads,' he said, 'let's go!' Luke had been in a few scuffles playing football, but he hadn't been in a street fight in his life. Not having ever been in a fight and not knowing how to fight, however, are two very different things. He let the biggest guy push him and used the force to circle round to flank the thugs; that way it could only ever be one on one. If another thug tried to get alongside the big guy, Luke would flank again; he kept moving, always engaging the biggest guy. He figured if he could drop him, the others would turn tail and run.

'Let's have it then, princess,' he taunted; he knew if he could get the big guy to throw the first punch, whatever he did would be classed – quite rightly – as self-defence. Sure enough, the thug obliged and swung a sharp right; Luke leaned away from it and let it whip past his nose. Before he'd even finished his swing, Luke nailed him with a straight left to the cheek, followed by a right hook to the middle of his face. Then he stepped back and waited for the thug to come at him again.

In both football and boxing training Luke had found you always backed the guy who knew how to take a hit and keep coming. Luke was definitely that guy, although in this instance he didn't have to be; as the thug swung again, Luke dodged, and then loaded up with a huge right that turned his nose and dropped him to the ground. There were three more of them still to come at him, so Luke gave the downed guy another one to make sure he stayed down; it was intended more as a sign to the others to go home than to punish the guy on the deck.

He turned to face the others and saw the tactic had worked; they were backing away. Luke stood his ground and let them go; he reckoned he'd just saved some kid a beating.

'What's going on?' Patty called as he and Johnny ran back to their friends. 'We were halfway down the street when we heard a commotion.'

'Luke's just taught one of those thugs a lesson,' said Barnaby, as he got up from his seat on the bench. He clapped Luke on the back. 'Come on, time we all went home.' As the friends walked towards Luke's place, he explained to them what had happened.

'What's that racket?' said Johnny, just as Luke was finishing his account. 'It sounds like a herd of elephants!'

Luke looked: the bloke he'd thumped was coming back and he had a small army of mates with him, their feet thudding on the pavement as they drew closer.

'You!' shouted the guy at the front when he saw them turn to look. 'Come here, you!' He pointed at Luke.

'There must be twenty of them,' said Luke. 'Christ, run!'

The four friends took to their heels, and Luke and Patty bolted down the hill, back towards the nightclub they'd considered going to earlier. Patty turned to see where the other two were and saw that Barnaby and Johnny had been surrounded.

Meanwhile the guys who'd chased after Patty and Luke were squaring up to them. Realising they were close to the nightclub, Patty bolted over the road and then saw the guys turn and run away as the nightclub bouncers ran out to break up the fight. Back up the road, Barnaby was keen to defuse the situation

'Look, why don't we all just calm down,' he said. He turned full circle as he spoke, speaking to all of them, not leaving his back to anyone for too long.

'There's no need for any of this,' Barnaby heard Johnny say, although he could hardly see him for the crush of bodies; the gang had got in between them and split them up. Before Johnny could say anything else he was king hit from behind; the crowd suddenly scattered and Johnny fell to the ground, unconscious. Barnaby fought to get to him as he saw a couple of guys start kicking his friend while he was down and out. He managed to shove them away and he saw Johnny's eyes flicker open, then there was a flash of bright pain, the lights went out and Barnaby hit the deck.

Luke and Patty ran up to the group and saw their friends being kicked into by at least ten thick set thugs, Luke shoved two of the attackers away as the nightclub bouncers and security from a local bar raced up and formed a protective circle around the two men on the ground.

Johnny was struggling to get to his feet and Patty was helping him. There was blood everywhere; his face had taken a hell of a pounding. Barnaby was still flat out. Luke knelt beside him, his heart in his mouth, and felt for a pulse.

'Thank god,' he muttered when he found one. Barnaby started to come round to find Luke kneeling over him.

'Mate? You okay?'

Cautiously, Barnaby sat up; his head was throbbing. 'How long was I out?' he asked.

Luke shrugged. 'Couple of minutes, I reckon. How's your head?'

'Hurts like bloody hell.' Barnaby put his hand to the back of his head and was relieved to find there was no broken skin. 'What happened?'

'I don't know, mate. I got back and they were kicking in to you and Johnny.' 'Johnny got king hit, then they lashed into him. Where is he? Is he okay?'

'I think so. Covered in blood, though.'

Barnaby spotted Patty and Johnny through the crowd; they were both on their feet, so that was a good sign.

The police arrived and after Luke explained what had happened and a few others told them what they knew, they took several of the pack of thugs away.

By then Barnaby was up on his feet.

'We need to get you to the hospital to get checked out,' Luke said.

'No, I'll be alright, mate. No need.'

'Mate, you were out cold, there were guys kicking you in the head. I really think you should go to the hospital.'

'I feel okay. Must be used to getting knocked out through playing footy.' Barnaby looked around. 'Where's Patty and Johnny?'

'Johnny went off in an ambulance to get checked out; Patty went with him.' Luke tried again. 'You should go, too.'

'Nah. Come on, we need to go to the police station to make statements.'

***

After that night life went on as usual; work, study, family, friends, all the normal stuff people deal with day to day. Two days later, on Saturday, Barnaby went to play football as usual and captained Sydney AFL representative team to victory over the Riverina AFL representative team.

The following Tuesday and Thursday nights he had his regular footy training and after Thursday night training he went to the pub for a few beers with his team mates; four days later he woke up in hospital wondering what on earth had happened.

CHAPTER 1:
A 'normal' life begins

Barnaby Howarth never wanted anything more than to be an ordinary man, working for a living, paying his taxes and playing footy on the weekends, with the hope of one day meeting someone special and enjoying a future together…he reckoned that would be more than enough to make him happy. It didn't seem a lot to ask; in fact, it sounded a lot like his parents' life, and if he could have a happy life with the girl he loved, he would be a happy man.

Denise and Ross Howarth and their four kids lived in Thornleigh, a suburb of Sydney in New South Wales. Barnaby was the middle one of three boys; Adam was the eldest and Lachlan the youngest. The baby of the family was their little sister, Ashley, and the four youngsters and their parents were a close knit group.

When Barnaby was six, he followed Adam into Warrawee Primary School and a couple of years later Lachlan joined them. Barnaby loved school, it was an atmosphere in which he excelled, and by the time Adam moved on to The Hills Grammar School, Barnaby was captain of Patterson House. He was a natural leader, something that was recognised from an early age, and during his time at The Hills Grammar School, he moved up from house captain at Warrawee to school captain at Hills Grammar.

Sport was always a big deal for the Howarth family and when Barnaby was eight years old, his dad signed him up to play Aussie Rules football with the Pennant Hills Demons. It was thanks to the 'mighty Dees' that he learned how to kick a drop punt and how to knock the wind out of an opponent by jabbing the palm of his hand into their solar plexus. He also learned how to keep faith in your game plan – whether you're a hundred points up or a hundred points down, have faith in the plan and the result will take care of itself.

The boys often kicked a football around the garden together and Barnaby was always keen to pass on what he had learned to his siblings.

'You hold the ball like this,' he said to Lachlan one day, showing him, then passing him the ball. 'Then drop it, and kick it before it hits the ground. Go on, try it.'

Lachlan tried and missed, and Adam rolled his eyes.

'You were closer that time; have another go,' said Barnaby, running to get the ball.

'I'm hungry,' said Adam, 'I'm going in.' he pushed open the door to the kitchen, then said, 'Mum, is there any chocolate spread?'

'Yes, I bought a jar at the weekend when I went grocery shopping. It's just in the cupboard there.'

Adam opened the cupboard and looked. 'It's not here,' he said.

'Let me see.' Denise checked for herself, but sure enough, there was no jar of chocolate spread in the cupboard. She narrowed her eyes; she was pretty sure she knew what had happened. 'Barnaby?' she shouted. 'Come in here a moment, please.'

Barnaby dropped the football and ran in to see what his mum wanted. When he saw her and Adam peering into the cupboard, he stopped dead.

'Barnaby, the jar of chocolate spread I bought at the weekend has gone missing. Do you know anything about that?'

Barnaby hesitated before saying, 'I only meant to have a little bit of it.'

'And how much did you have?'

'You ate the bloody jar again, didn't you!' exclaimed Adam.

'Adam Howarth, I will not have language like that in this house!'

'I'm sorry, Mum, but he's a gannet. Nobody else stands a chance.'

Denise was still annoyed with Adam, so Barnaby seized his chance to escape. 'I'm going back outside; I'm teaching Lachlan to kick a drop punt. I'm sorry about the chocolate spread, it won't happen again, Mum, honest!'

Denise shook her head. Barnaby was always hungry, when they went to McDonald's he had to have an extra six chicken nuggets on top of the standard portion of twenty or it didn't fill him up, but that was no excuse. Mind you, it didn't excuse Adam, either. She'd have to keep an eye on her two eldest boys!

Dinner that evening was Lachlan's favourite, lasagne, and he piled up his plate and ate his fill, then had a double helping of trifle for pudding. When he finally put down his spoon and everyone had

3

finished, Ross said, 'Okay, kids, you're excused. You can leave the table.'

'Do your fattest!' Lachlan cried, sure he would win the competition that night, and the boys jumped up from their seats, stood side by side, lifted their shirts and stuck out their bellies. Denise and Ross left them to it and started clearing the dishes through to the kitchen.

'I win,' shouted Barnaby, and he did a lap of honour around the dining table.

Lachlan looked crestfallen; 'I ate heaps at dinner, I was sure I'd win this time,' he said to Adam.

Adam ruffled his hair; 'Don't get upset mate, he's unbeatable. He's like a bloody dustbin!'

'Adam Howarth!' shouted Denise from the kitchen.

'And Mum's got ears like a bloody bat,' Adam whispered.

'I heard that. Enough, do you hear? Come and help with the washing up!'

'Yes, Mum, coming,' he said, rolling his eyes at Lachlan as he went.

'And don't roll your eyes, either!'

***

Barnaby was happy growing up; he loved his family and was best friends with his brothers and sister. School was great fun, he had lots of friends and he wanted for nothing. He loved the challenges sport presented and thrived on always trying to be and do better than before. And while he always hoped he'd be able to meet a challenge if it was presented, he could never have anticipated what life had in store for him.

***

One day when Barnaby was fourteen, his mum drove him to the medical centre to get the results of a recent blood test.

'There must be an emergency,' said Denise as she pulled into a parking space. Barnaby looked out of the car window to see the doctor racing out of the building and into the car park. 'Must be serious; look at him go, he looks like he's being chased by an axe-wielding psycho!'

'He's heading straight for us,' said Denise. She climbed out of the car.

'Quick,' said the doctor, 'come on inside. I've got an ambulance coming for Barnaby.'

'Why do I need an ambulance?' said Barnaby, slamming the car door behind him hard enough to make the vehicle rock. Denise was too concerned to scold him for it; the doctor had her worried.

'Come on, quickly,' he said, and Denise and Barnaby hurried along behind as the doctor trotted back into his surgery.

'Right,' said Denise. 'What's up?'

'It's Barnaby's blood test results.' The doctor grabbed a sheet of paper from the desk. 'I couldn't believe my eyes when I read this. I rang up to check; I thought they must have made a mistake, but it's correct.'

'What does it say?' asked Barnaby.

'It says that your blood sugar level is 38; normal blood sugars are between 3.5 and 8, so yours is sky high, practically off the charts.'

'Is that bad?'

'Bad? It's dangerous. You need to be hospitalised immediately so we can get things under control.' He grabbed the phone on his desk when it rang, then said, 'The ambulance is here, guys. Come on, let's go.'

'I'll follow in the car,' Denise told Barnaby. 'I want to ring your dad and let him know what's happening.' She looked at the doctor. 'I'll see you there. Look after him, won't you?'

CHAPTER 2:
A diabetic life begins

Ross was at the office when Denise's phone call sent a bolt of shock right through him; he grabbed his car keys and headed straight for the hospital.

When he got there, he found Barnaby sitting up in bed with a grin on his face, looking absolutely fine.

'What's the drama?' he said, confused.

'I've got diabetes, Dad, I'm going to be in here all week.'

Well, that explains the grin, thought Ross; *a week in hospital means a week off school.* 'They don't keep people in hospital for no reason,' he said, glancing at Denise. 'There's obviously more to it.' Before she could answer, they were interrupted.

'Mr and Mrs Howarth? I'm Doctor Clark. Good to meet you.'

'You too,' said Ross, shaking the doctor's hand. 'What can you tell us?'

'Barnaby has type 1 diabetes; it's also known as juvenile or early-onset diabetes because it usually develops during a person's teenage years.'

'How has he got that?'

'It's caused by the failure of the pancreas to produce insulin, the hormone that regulates blood glucose levels. If the amount of glucose in the blood is too high, it can seriously damage the body's organs.'

'How do I regulate it?' asked Barnaby.

7

'You'll need to take insulin injections for the rest of your life to make sure that your blood glucose levels stay balanced. Unless they find a cure, that is. You'll also have to watch what you eat, take regular exercise and have regular blood tests, to keep an eye on things.'

Barnaby nodded; that didn't sound too bad.

***

At home that evening, Ross and Denise got the other three kids together to explain to them what was happening to their brother. Denise's background in nursing was a great help at the time and she explained to the children what diabetes was and what food and drink Barnaby would have to avoid.

'You mean he can't have chocolate ever again?' asked Ashley, horrified at the prospect.

'He won't be able to eat a whole jar of chocolate spread, that's for sure,' said Adam. His comment masked the concern he felt for his brother's wellbeing.

'It's not just chocolate,' said Denise, and she went on to describe what they'd have to look for in the lists of ingredients on tinned and packaged foods to ensure Barnaby's diet didn't include sugar and fatty foods.

'Look,' said Adam, 'I don't know how you lot feel about this, but I don't want my brother to feel that he's different and can't eat the same things that we do. I think we should all change our diet and eat and drink the same as Barnaby.'

'How do you all feel about that?' Denise asked the other children.

'It makes sense, doesn't it?' said Lachlan.

'I think we should do it,' agreed Ashley, 'apart from chocolate.'

Afterwards Ross took Adam to one side. 'What you said in the family meeting was very mature, Adam, it showed real love and support for your brother. I'm proud of you, son.'

'Thanks, Dad. I'm just really worried about Barnaby, you know? And I reckon if we don't have any of the wrong stuff in the house, he can't make a mistake.'

***

For Barnaby, the news that he was diabetic was followed by one of the steepest learning curves of his life, as the condition and how to manage it were explained to him.

While he was in hospital, he met the man who was to become a mainstay of his learning and his treatment, endocrinologist Doctor John Carter.

As Doctor Carter explained the first time the two met, 'Endocrinology deals with the diagnosis and treatment of diseases related to hormones.'

'Like insulin,' said Barnaby.

'Exactly. Doctors like me are trained to diagnose and treat hormone imbalances and problems by helping to restore the normal balance.'

'So you'll help me sort out the whole business with the injections?'

'That and more besides. How are you feeling now that the news has had a bit of time to sink in?'

Barnaby sighed. 'I'll be honest, I'm starting to feel really worried.'

'That's understandable. Finding out you have an illness that means you're going to have to be careful for the rest of your life would worry anyone.'

'It's not the illness so much as what it might mean ... I'm concerned about the changes I'll have to make.'

'In what way?'

'Well, I love playing sport and going out with my mates and up to now I've been able to do that whenever I wanted. I don't want to lose that freedom. I don't want to be wrapped in cotton wool and monitored like a science experiment for the rest of my life. I don't want to have to become dependent on other people to help me to survive. You know?'

Doctor Carter nodded. 'Yes, I understand, and I'll be speaking with your parents so I can put a word in for you about that. As for being dependent on others, part of what I'm going to be teaching you is how to be self-reliant when it comes to managing your diabetes.' He sat back in his chair. 'Do you know who Dale Weightman is?'

Barnaby nodded.

'How about Steve Renouf, Gary Hall Jr and Marcia Hines?'

'Yes, of course.' Barnaby recognised all the names immediately, they were all champions in their field. Dale 'Flea' Weightman is a former Australian rules footballer; Stephen Renouf is an Australian former professional rugby league footballer; Gary Hall Jr is an American swimmer who won ten Olympic medals and Marcia Hines is an Australian vocalist, actress and TV personality.

'Well, what you probably don't know is that each and every one of them is a diabetic.'

'So it doesn't have to hold you back,' said Barnaby, his brain working overtime.

'No, it doesn't; but you have to treat the condition with respect and take care of yourself.'

'I've learned heaps about diabetes this week. It seems to me that the beauty of it is that even though I'm ill, I can still run, walk, jump, swim, talk, see, hear, laugh and think just the same as I could before. I'll have to be careful, but I don't have to miss out.'

'I'm glad you're starting to get your head around what diabetes does and doesn't have to mean in your life,' said Doctor Carter, 'but don't get blasé, Barnaby. Make sure you establish a routine – keep to the right diet, drink in moderation when you're old enough, and inject insulin four times a day – and make sure you stick to it. Make it second nature to do what's best for your health. I know it can be challenging, especially for someone who's so young, but you must do it.'

'I will, I promise, although I can't guarantee I won't mess up occasionally.'

'Occasionally is okay, just make sure it doesn't become the norm.' Doctor Carter sat forward in his chair to emphasise his point. 'Just two floors below where we are now there's a young woman, a diabetic, who may or may not survive. She's only thirty-four but for the last fifteen years or so she's put her social life before her health and now she's paying the price. Diabetes can be managed – it doesn't have to stop you living life to the full or getting to the top of your

11

field – but you must treat it with respect or it can kill you. Never forget that.'

***

Within a week of his release from hospital, Barnaby was thrown in at the deep end with a basketball tournament. Over the course of the weekend, Barnaby's team played three games. He suffered his first hypoglycaemic episode, when his blood sugar fell too low, at dinner on the first night, and a high blood sugar level during the second game left him thirsty and fatigued, but all things considered, his first physically demanding venture since being diagnosed went pretty smoothly, which was a huge relief. He might not yet have a firm grasp on his diabetes control, but his condition wasn't going to hold him back.

The level of uncertainty about what he could realistically achieve in life as a diabetic had been daunting, but that weekend reassured him that he was still the one in charge, still the one to decide how far he got in life. Sure, diabetes was always going to have to be a consideration, but it thankfully didn't have to be a restriction.

***

If the reassurance of the basketball tournament was a comfort, the reaction of his classmates when he got back to school was less encouraging. They seemed reluctant to talk to him and while he tried to stay relaxed and open about his diagnosis, others seemed determined to avoid the subject; it made them distinctly uneasy.

'It's weird, Mum,' Barnaby confided, 'it's not that they ignore me exactly, but instead of treating me like their friend, they act like we've just met.'

'Are they mean to you?'

'No, they still talk to me, but they're … polite.'

'What, your schoolmates are polite to you?' Denise laughed. 'That must be scary!'

'Yeah, it's freaky.'

'What are you going to do about it?'

'I don't know, but I'll have to come up with something. I just want things back the way they were, you know?'

Next day, when it was time for his insulin injection – or 'stabbing', as he thought of it – he put up his hand and asked to be excused, then went to the bathroom and 'stabbed' there. It was a private thing, deeply personal, and he didn't need an audience for that, especially an audience of people who couldn't even bring themselves to talk to him about his condition.

As Barnaby put his gear back in the case after administering the injection, he had a moment of clarity; if he wanted people to be more accepting of his condition and to talk to him about it, then he'd have to make the first move and be more open about it. People's reluctance to talk was driven by a fear of the unknown and if he 'stabbed' in private, his condition would remain unknown and nothing would ever change. Seeking privacy was counter-intuitive.

Next day, when it was time to 'stab' Barnaby didn't put up his hand and he didn't ask to be excused; he took out his kit, laid out what he needed on the desk, and administered his injection.

'What's that you're doing?' one of his classmates asked him, staring in fascination. 'Are you on drugs?'

'Yes,' said Barnaby, 'for the rest of my life.'

'Does it hurt?'

Barnaby shrugged. 'You get used to it.'

'What is it you're injecting?'

'Insulin.' He went on to explain a bit more about his condition and while stabbing in public caused a bit of a stir for the first week or two, once people had seen him do it a few times the novelty wore off and no one even seemed to notice.

It had only been a few weeks since his initial diagnosis, but Barnaby was getting in to the swing of things when it came to managing his diabetes. He'd accepted he'd have to live with it – there was no way he could change things, after all – and he was working out a strategy for that. He was actually feeling relieved, because he'd already tested the boundaries and established that diabetes wasn't the kind of medical condition that could hold him back. Sure, there'd be some tough times ahead, but there'd undoubtedly be tough times even without diabetes.

As it was he could still play basketball, study and have fun with his friends.

He'd have to be careful what he ate and drank, and also stab himself with a needle a few times every day, but that was all stuff he could manage. It would be fine; he could handle it.

***

14

A full year after being diagnosed with diabetes, Barnaby dashed in from school, said a quick hello to his parents, dumped his school bag at the foot of the stairs and headed through to the TV room.

'Barnaby? Take that bag upstairs, please,' his mum shouted.

'Later!' He flicked on the set for Astro Boy; Brutus had Astro cornered and was about to kill him – things were critical and he couldn't miss a second of it!

'Now!' came back the reply. Barnaby wondered if Mum was putting her foot down because Dad was home; she normally gave up after scolding him once and let him watch TV before he took his things up to his room.

'Oh, Mum, can't it wait?'

'No, it can't. Jump to it, young man. Now!'

Following a last glance at Astro's desperate plight, Barnaby ran upstairs as fast as he could, snagging his school bag on the way, not wanting to miss a second more than he had to of Astro's struggle for survival. As he was heading down the corridor to his room he noticed that both his parents were standing at the bottom of the stairs watching … and that, coupled with his dad being home and his mum being insistent about the school bag, added up to something very odd.

When he got into his room he stopped dead in his tracks: sitting on his bed was a brand new stereo system! He dropped his school bag and ran over to look at it; it was fantastic, exactly what he would have chosen for himself. He found a note from his mum attached to it and grinned when he read it: 'If you ever wake us up in the middle of the night with this, we'll file all your needles blunt!' He turned to see his folks standing in the doorway, smiling at him.

'Thanks so much, this is awesome,' he said, hugging them. 'Wow, I knew you were up to something, but I didn't expect anything like this!'

'You're welcome. You've done so well this past year, you deserve it,' his dad said. 'We're proud of you, Barnaby.'

'But I meant what I said about the needles,' his mum added, laughing.

Barnaby was fifteen; he'd just completed the first year of his journey as a diabetic, as marked by his parents' very generous gift, and he still had a lot of living to do. He'd rather not have been diabetic, but that wasn't his choice – and if he knew one thing for sure, it was that he wouldn't let it hold him back, ever.

He'd accepted the challenge, met it head on and was dealing with it. If that was the worst card life dealt him, then he reckoned things wouldn't be so bad.

CHAPTER 3:
Life as a diabetic Sydney Swan

A few years had passed since Barnaby had been diagnosed diabetic and he and Adam were kicking a footy around in the garden.

'Hey, Barnaby,' Adam said, 'what are your plans for when you leave school?'

Barnaby shrugged. 'I've no firm plans yet. I'll think of something, though.'

He dropped the ball on to his foot and booted it back to Adam.

'You'd better hurry up,' said Adam, running for the ball, 'your last day will be here before you know it. Mine really caught me by surprise.'

Barnaby just nodded; he knew all too well that the time was nigh to make a decision, but he was torn. While he was fully confident that he wouldn't allow his diabetes to hold him back at all, he wasn't sure how a potential employer might view his condition, and he'd have no choice but to tell them about it.

Besides which, he didn't really want a 'proper' job; he liked being active and outdoors. Work sounded too much like school, and school involved too much sitting down and watching the world through a window rather than being out in it. For that same reason, university was off the menu; he'd had enough of full time education for now.

In his heart of hearts, Barnaby knew that if he was going to do what he loved doing most, he had just two options open to him: play AFL with the

Sydney Swans or play AFL with a different team. The worrying thing was that he'd had no indication so far that any AFL club wanted him; it was increasingly looking like he'd have to come up with a third option, and that it would very likely involve getting a 'proper' job and sitting behind a desk for eight hours a day, five days a week. His heart sank at the prospect.

It was 1997, and the footy team Barnaby played for trained after the Sydney Swans at the SCG, the Sydney Cricket Ground, where the previous September Tony Lockett had kicked a point after the siren to defeat Essendon and put the Swans into their first AFL Grand Final since they had relocated to Sydney. They'd faced North Melbourne Football Club at Melbourne Cricket Ground later that month and, while Lockett acquitted himself well in that match too, they had been beaten by the other team.

After training one night, Barnaby walked out into the middle of the ground. Slowly he turned full circle, looking at all the empty seats and imagining them full, the stadium packed with fans yelling, screaming and chanting, the atmosphere electric, and he got goose bumps. The feeling was euphoric. The chants still echoing in his head, he bent down and plucked a few tufts of grass, then tucked them in to his wallet.

He knew what he wanted for his future: anything other than playing with the Swans was going to be a bitter pill to swallow, and any time he wanted to remember what his goal was, what he was working towards every time he trained and played, he just had to open his wallet and see those few tufts of grass. They became his totem.

As the days and weeks slipped by, some of Barnaby's team mates started to get phone calls from AFL clubs about joining for the 1998 season, but the Howarth phone stayed stubbornly quiet, at least as far as calls from AFL clubs was concerned.

As it got towards the end of the year, Barnaby was starting to steel himself for the awful reality of having to accept option three; traditional employment. He was stoical: he had, after all, faced up to fears and unwelcome realities before and he'd beaten them every time; this would be no exception. By the time he answered the phone one day late in 1997, he had no hopes or expectations about who it might be on the other end of the line.

'Hi,' he said.

'Hello, could I speak with Barnaby Howarth, please?'

'This is Barnaby Howarth. Who's calling?'

'My name is Colin Seery, I'm calling from the Sydney Swans.'

Barnaby's heart leapt in his chest. 'Okay,' he said, keeping his voice steady.

'We'd like you to join us for pre-season training, if you're interested.'

Barnaby didn't need to hear any more. 'Yes,' he said, 'I'm interested, absolutely. When do we start?'

'So when do you start?' Denise asked him later as he shared the news with the family over dinner.

'November. There'll be thirty of us trying out for nine spots, so there's no guarantee of a contract, but it's a chance.'

'Training with the Sydney Swans,' said Lachlan. 'That's ace.'

'Well done, son,' said Ross; 'I'm proud of you.'
'We all are,' said Denise. 'Well done.'

***

If Barnaby was nervous about joining the Swans for pre-season training, every shred of doubt disappeared when he arrived on his first day: there were no desks, computers, meeting rooms or photocopiers to be seen, just seventy players, the team coaches, some water bottles and a few bags of footballs. As far as he was concerned, it was the perfect office!

It was still hard work, though, and the training was regimented and tough.

There were weights five times a week, skills training after every running session and regular football training every other day; the rest of the time, the job was to stay as fit and become as skilful as possible.

Barnaby got stuck in and did the best he could. He knew the odds were against him – he was aiming to be one of nine chosen out of thirty hopefuls, after all – but if there was one thing he was used to, it was uncertainty. As the days and weeks went by and more and more people were called in by head coach Rodney Eade and cut from the list, he kept the words he'd heard so often from the Pennant Hills footy coach, Danny Ryan, in his head: focus on the game plan and the result will take care of itself.

Then one day Rodney Eade called him over. As Barnaby walked towards the coach, his future hung in the balance. He had no idea what to expect, he only knew he'd given it his best shot.

'Yes, Coach?' he said.

Rodney Eade held out his hand. 'Congratulations, Barnaby,' he said, 'you've made the team. Well done, and welcome to the Swans.'

Barnaby grasped the coach's hand and shook it enthusiastically. 'Really? No kidding? Thanks, Coach!'

Barnaby had done it! Another hurdle cleared and something else diabetes hadn't been able to hold him back from achieving. He was a full time professional athlete.

There were smiles all round when he broke the news to the family that night over dinner, although Ashley was puzzled at first.

'How can playing football be a job? You only play once a week. Dad goes to the office every day. What do you do?'

'There's a lot more to it than the fixtures, Ashley,' said Barnaby. 'It's now my full time job to stay fit and to practise footy, so I get my skills as good as they can be.'

'You do that anyway.'

'Yeah, and now I'm getting paid for it,' he said, grinning. 'Life couldn't be better; I'm going to be living the dream.'

Barnaby turned up for training on the first day he was a full member of the Sydney Swans and headed into the locker room; he could hardly believe he was one of the gang and yet there he was, getting ready to start training and playing footy alongside such 'elder statesmen' as Paul Roos and Tony Lockett. It was all he could do not to call them 'Sir'!

As time passed and he settled into the routine of being a professional athlete, he began to realise they were just like him; ordinary blokes who were passionate about football and lucky enough to be exceptionally good at it.

As the squad went back into the locker rooms one afternoon after training, Barnaby grabbed his diabetes kit from his locker. Taking a seat in a corner of the room – neither hiding nor taking centre stage – he first checked his blood sugar level, then administered an insulin injection. For all his quiet approach to the task, he was noticed and he looked up to see two of his team mates watching what he was doing.

Tony 'Plugger' Lockett looked down at the needle, then back up at Barnaby. 'Fuck that,' he said, shaking his head.

Swans captain Paul Kelly was the other observer. He'd been voted the AFL's most courageous player three times, and yet he looked at Barnaby and what he was doing and said, 'You're a braver bloke than me.'

The more time Barnaby spent with the other players and the better he got to know them, the more comfortable he felt telling other people that he was an AFL footballer. His confidence was growing and it was reflected in his performance on the field, as his skills were honed by training and playing alongside such dedicated and talented professionals as his team mates.

In round nine of the AFL season, the Sydney Swans faced Richmond and Barnaby's efforts and progress were acknowledged when he was named one of the Swans' best players of the match. It might not have meant cash prizes, or his name in lights or a history book, but to Barnaby it meant even more than that; it was recognition of his outstanding performance in that particular game, and he was proud to be recognised.

Buoyed by his achievements, Barnaby was full of confidence as the team arrived at the Melbourne Cricket Ground to play against Collingwood a short time afterwards.

As they piled off the team coach and into the changing room at the 'G'; Barnaby was filled with excitement. He had a good feeling about the match and he couldn't wait to get his hands on the football. He changed in double quick time and fidgeted until it was time to run out onto the field. He was full of energy and confidence, determined to show everyone there what he was capable of.

From his position in the Swans backline, he spotted a chance to kick a goal, so he took off to the forward line to try to make it pay off. As he got there, one of his team mates had the ball, but he had his back to the goal; Barnaby raced past him, took the hand pass and kicked a goal from thirty metres out. The crowd went wild as the ball passed between the posts!

If Barnaby had felt bullet proof before scoring that goal, he was now completely indestructible; he felt as though he could take on the world. Even if his world should spiral into oblivion, he could always say he'd kicked a goal on the MCG. It was a great achievement, and a moment he'd never forget.

When the season came to an end, Barnaby was once more in a place of uncertainty. Had he done enough to be kept on for the following season?

He wasn't confident, but then again he hadn't been confident the year before. And like the year before, it was now a waiting game.

Sure enough, the call finally came to go and see head coach Rodney Eade and learn his fate. Sadly for Barnaby, his worst fears were realised and he was released by the Swans after one season.

***

Barnaby might no longer have been on the Swans' list, but he still had one more obligation to fulfil, and it was one he was looking forward to: an end of season trip to Phuket in Thailand.

Phuket is an island paradise situated off the west coast of Thailand in the Andaman Sea, connected to the mainland by two bridges. The white sandy beaches, clear turquoise seas and warm, sunny weather make it an ideal holiday spot.

In between visits to the beach, trips to see local tourist attractions and sampling the delicious local cuisine, the players relaxed at the hotel. One afternoon while sitting by the hotel pool Barnaby and Troy Luff got talking.

'So,' said Troy, 'what are you going to do next? After the Swans, I mean?'

'Believe it or not, I'm going to write a book.'

'Yeah? What sort of book?'

'I want to write something to help people to understand diabetes better, and to help diabetics cope with their illness.'

'What made you decide to do that?'

'It was something that happened a few years ago.' Barnaby took a sip of his drink. 'I was about seventeen and I'd been living with diabetes for four years or so. I was pretty much on top of it. I mean, I'd had my ups and downs, but I'd come to terms with it and I wasn't letting my condition hold me back.'

'I'll say. You've done more with diabetes than most people manage to do without it. I remember the first time I saw you injecting; that must all take a bit of getting used to.'

'For sure, but I've had a lot of help and support.'

'So what was it that happened to make you want to write a book about it?'

'There was this kid, Jordan. He was thirteen and diabetic, and he was having a rough time. His mum asked me to talk to him, sort of like a big brother, you know?'

Troy nodded.

'Anyway, I tried, but I didn't really know what to say. He was a funny little spud … he had a squeaky voice I thought he was putting on, so I probably wasn't as sympathetic as I could have been to start with, then I realised it was real, poor bugger. He had nothing going for him.'

'Yeah, I remember kids like that from school. There's nothing you can do, they just have to find their own way, you know?'

Barnaby nodded, realising the truth of it. 'I spoke to him a couple of times, but the thing I remember most clearly is how despondent he and his mum were about his diagnosis. It was like someone had said to him, "You're going to die," and he'd said, "Oh, okay, then," and he just lay down to wait for it to happen. There was no fight in him, no hope.'

'How did you feel when you were diagnosed?'

'Anxious, confused, a bit frightened, too, if I'm honest. But right away I learned about diabetics who'd done well despite their illness, like Dale Weightman, Marcia Hines and Steve Renouf. I saw it as a hurdle, not a brick wall. After I spoke to Jordan, I started researching the subject on the Internet and when I read other people's stories I realised how lucky I'd been; a lot of people are just told that if they don't look after themselves, they'll die.'

'That's hardly going to brighten your day.'

'Exactly! So, now I want to pay some of that back. I want to help diabetic kids see that while they do have to learn to live with it, they don't have to let diabetes hold them back.' He snorted. 'And make amends for being rubbish at helping Jordan! He's my inspiration, really.'

'Good on ya, mate, I hope it all works out.'

'Thanks.' Barnaby sipped his drink. 'What about you, though? How did you enjoy your travels?' Before joining his friends in Thailand, Troy had been holidaying in Europe and Barnaby was keen to know more.

'It was fantastic,' Troy said, grinning, 'I had a whale of a time.'

'Where did you go?'

'Oh, all over. London, Paris, Rome … I had a terrific trip.'

'What was London like? What did you get up to?'

'London was great fun. I did the usual tourist stuff, but would you believe there's an Aussie pub there that shows twenty-four hour sports? The only time there's no AFL is when there's a rugby union test match on.'

'Sounds sensible to me. Where did you go after that?'

'Paris, the city of light. It was fantastic, a real experience.'

'How did you get on with the language?'

'Most places there's someone who speaks English. I got a bit sick of the food in Paris, mind.'

'How come?'

'There was no one who spoke English around to translate for me; all I knew how to ask for in French was a ham and cheese crepe.' Troy grinned. 'I think I very nearly overdosed on them.'

'Idiot!'

'Then it was on to Rome. It's an amazing city, just beautiful. You see modern buildings standing right alongside ancient Roman ruins. One of the highlights of my trip was the visit to the Coliseum; you'd love it, it's just like an ancient version of Melbourne Cricket Ground.'

'No kidding!'

'Yeah, really. And the atmosphere … just amazing, such a sense of history. Knowing you're treading a path others have walked for thousands of years. It gives you a sense of perspective.'

Barnaby had seen pictures of the Coliseum in print and on TV, but as good as they were, they couldn't impart the atmosphere or give a sense of place; that was something you could only get by being there.

'Come on,' Troy said, 'let's go and find the others, see what we're doing tonight.' Barnaby got up and followed along behind Troy. He was distracted, still thinking about the Coliseum. As Troy had said, feet had trodden that ground for thousands of years. Not only that, the feet of sportsmen like himself, contenders in their own version of the MCG, had raced over it, striving for victory, in some cases fighting to survive. The very stone was steeped in sweat and blood, the roar of the crowd had echoed around the now silent, ruined walls for centuries; the sense of history must be palpable.

Barnaby was beginning to get itchy feet as he realised how little of the world he'd actually seen. Fair enough, he'd been to New Zealand and now Thailand, too, but it was a big old world and there was a lot more to it; London Bridge, The Swiss Alps, New York, the Rockies, even the Eiffel Tower, while eating a ham and cheese crepe … they were all there waiting for him.

He realised he wanted to travel more widely, to see the world for himself, and while he wasn't sure how easy that would be as a diabetic, he knew there was only one way to find out.

CHAPTER 4:
Flying solo

Barnaby was having dinner with the family one night later that year when he said, 'I've got some news. I'm going to go travelling round Europe.'

'Yeah? Who with?' asked Adam.

'Just on my own.'

'That doesn't sound like much fun,' said Lachlan.

'You got no mates?' said Adam, grinning.

Barnaby grinned back. 'Okay, then, on my own, but with other people; I've booked a place on a Contiki tour, so there'll be a group of us. We're going to hit ten countries in sixteen days, so it'll be pretty intense.'

Lachlan gave a low whistle. 'That's some ground you're going to cover!'

'Yeah, that's for sure. I'm going to see all the sights, though; it'll be great.'

'Can I come?' asked Ashley. 'I want to go to Europe. I especially want to see London.'

'You're too young,' said Barnaby. 'You can go when you're older.'

'I will,' she said. 'In fact, I might go and live there one day.'

'Oh, really?' teased Adam.

'Yes, really,' said Ashley, sticking her chin out. 'I'm going to be an international jet setter.'

'Jet lagger, more like.'

'Just rewind a minute there, son,' said Ross, cutting through the banter to focus on what was important. 'How on earth will you manage your condition on a long trip like that?'

'I've thought it all out,' Barnaby said. 'I'm going to take double the amount of stuff I need for the whole trip and split it between two separate bags, so if one gets lost, I'll still have the other. That way there's no chance I'll be left high and dry with no supplies.'

'Just make sure you don't lose them both,' said Denise.

'I'm not planning on losing either of them, I'm just being extra careful.'

'Will they let you through Customs with a load of drugs and needles?' asked Lachlan.

'I hadn't even thought of that,' said Denise.

'Well, luckily I did and I've been finding out about that, too. Even though it's for a medical condition, they get pretty jumpy about stuff like that. I've spoken to Doctor Carter and he's going to give me a letter explaining it's all necessary. I'm already stockpiling supplies so I can be sure I have enough.'

'Some of the places you're going, they don't even speak English, Barnaby,' said Denise. 'What will you do if something happens and you need help? How will you be able to tell them what the problem is?'

'Honestly, Mum, don't worry! I've done some research on everywhere I'm planning to visit. For every country, I've got a couple of places where I can get supplies in an emergency and I'm learning how to say "I am a diabetic" in the language of every country I'm going to.'

'Say it in French,' said Ashley, grinning.

'Je suis diabétique.'

'German.'

'Ich bin diabetiker.'

'Italian.'

'Io sono un diabetico.'

'Okay, we get the picture. You've thought it all through and you're well organised,' said Denise, smiling.

Barnaby grinned. 'I take after you, Mum; of course I'm well organised! And I keep telling you, diabetes is a condition that doesn't have to stop me doing anything. I just have to take a little care, that's all.'

***

Towards the end of 1999, after much organising and planning, Barnaby met up with his fellow travellers and they flew to London for the first leg of their tour of Europe. It was autumn in the northern hemisphere and the days were becoming cooler, the nights drawing in, but that just added to the experience. The tour was non-stop, all sixteen days packed with new experiences, new friends, and lots of fun.

In London he saw Tower Bridge and Buckingham Palace, shopped on Oxford Street and kicked through piles of red and brown leaves in Hyde Park to stand looking up at the statue of Peter Pan.

On the shores of Lake Lucerne, he shared Swiss chocolate with his fellow travellers as they chatted and gazed at the majestic snow-topped Alps, dominating the skyline in the distance.

He drank schnapps in Austria and ate pasta in Italy; in Germany he saw the biggest cuckoo clock and the biggest beer stein in the world, then drank beer out of a boot.

In France, he raided a lolly shop in Lyon, then moved on to Paris and saw the Eiffel Tower and the Champs Elysees; remembering Troy and his experiences when he was travelling, he even ordered a ham and cheese crepe – in French – in Paris.

Through it all, Barnaby made the most of every experience, in spite of his condition. He was careful to monitor his blood sugar levels, so that he could enjoy himself without taking risks; he kept his bags and his medical supplies safe; and he was asked only once at Customs for the letter from Doctor Carter.

By the time he got home again, his mind was buzzing. He had some incredible memories and didn't need asking twice to share them. The experience had been amazing, it had opened his eyes and his mind to the reality of the rest of the world and all he wanted to do was talk about it; how it had been, how it had changed him. He started taking an interest in international affairs, having previously not been interested in the world outside of Sydney, never mind Australia.

***

The European trip had shown Barnaby that travelling with a group was a great way to see the world and to get a taste for those countries he'd like to see again, and so he lost no time in booking himself on a five month round the world trip.

'What countries are you going to this time,' asked Ashley, excited on his behalf. 'Canada for three months, then a week in New York, three days in Paris, five days in Barcelona, three days in Nice, and a week in Switzerland. From there I go to Vienna, just for one night though; that's where I pick up my flight to Nepal.'

'Nepal!'

'Yup. I'm going to Kathmandu; I'll be in Nepal for three weeks, during which I'll be trekking in the Himalayas for sixteen days. Then it's home via Bangkok.

It'll be amazing.'

Ross and Denise exchanged a look. 'It will be amazing,' said Ross, 'but are you sure it's wise?'

'Your dad's right,' said Denise. 'It's one thing going to Europe for two or three weeks, but five months? What happens if you're trekking in the Himalayas and something happens? What will you do then?'

'I learned a lot on my last trip. I'll be well prepared and I'll be really careful. Honestly, don't worry; I'll be fine.'

'Just make sure you keep in touch. I know you've always been determined not to let your condition slow you down or stop you doing anything, but promise me you'll be careful.'

'I will, I promise.'

***

The first stop was Calgary in Canada, and Barnaby soon realised the implications of being there.

'Hey,' he said to Pete, one of his fellow travellers and fast becoming a friend, 'we're going to be in North America for Halloween.'

'Fantastic!' Pete said, 'Let's get costumes and go trick or treating.'

'Seriously?' said Jim, who'd overheard the conversation. 'Isn't it just for kids?'

'Kids and tourists, I reckon,' said Barnaby. 'Are you up for it?' Seeing he had an audience, he said, 'Anyone else fancy it?' Half a dozen voices confirmed they did.

'Great!' said Barnaby. 'We'll make an event of it.'

As soon as they were booked into the hotel, Barnaby set about finding a fancy dress shop and arranging a visit to it for his fellow trick or treaters. A couple of days later, they all made their way there and spent some time looking through the outfits and deciding what to wear. His mind made up, Barnaby snagged a costume off the rack and disappeared into a changing room.

'What do you think?' he asked as he stepped out in his chosen outfit.

'Fantastic!' said Pete, laughing. 'Don't cross the streams!'

He twirled his black cloak, showing the red lining, then bared his fangs. 'What do you reckon to my outfit?'

'Dracula … a classic. Love it.'

They were soon joined by another Ghostbuster, Hannibal Lecter, a mummy, Shrek, and

Frankenstein's monster, complete with bolt through the neck.

They had a great evening, roaming the streets, trick or treating and collecting sweets and chocolates. By the time they headed back to the hotel, Barnaby had a bag full of lollies and a belly full of sugar; he'd had a great time, but it had been hard not to indulge his sweet tooth even more than he had done. Checking his blood sugar level, it was fifteen; high, but it could have been a lot worse, and it was worth it to have had such a brilliant night.

Next day he felt guilty about his Halloween indulgence, so he decided to go for a run. Since they'd first met in Calgary at the start of the world tour, he and Pete had often gone running together, but on this occasion he wanted time to think. Travelling had not only broadened his mind, it had opened it up to a host of possibilities, and being freed from the regular day-to-day routine had allowed him to take a step back and think deeply about his life and his future.

As he ran, the regular rhythm of his feet as they hit the snow-covered pavements provided a backdrop to his thoughts. The voice of Ron Barassi, AFL Hall of Fame player and coach, echoed in his head: 'There's no disgrace in failing. The only disgrace is if you only half try, or three quarters try, or ninety-nine per cent try.'

With those words in mind, he looked back over his life so far with clarity and brutal honesty, and decided he didn't altogether like what he saw. He cast his mind forward and, like Jacob Marley when presented with the ghost of Christmas future, saw his life laid out in front of him and realised that if he didn't take action, he'd have to learn to live for the rest of his days with the regret that he hadn't tried hard enough to make it into the AFL. Being completely candid, he could see that during his time with the Swans he had given it maybe seventy-five per cent, not the full hundred; that's why Rodney Eade had let him go. He hadn't lacked talent, he had lacked commitment, caught up in the excitement of living the dream.

On that run, Barnaby made a life-affirming decision; he was going to make the most of the rest of his world trip and then, when he got home, he was going to give himself one last proper chance of playing AFL football.

The decision made, he felt as though a weight had been lifted from his shoulders and his thoughts turned to planning how he was going to make it all happen. To give himself a realistic chance of success, he'd have to move to Melbourne, which wasn't a thought he relished. But he knew that if he allowed that reluctance to take over and to stop him, he would be giving it less than one hundred per cent; so he adjusted his thinking and accepted that he'd be leaving Sydney shortly after he got back from his trip. Still, that was several months away, so he settled into his travels, intent on enjoying every experience.

After three glorious months in Canada, Barnaby took off for New York City.

It was a place he was very familiar with from movies and television shows so, with that in mind, he planned to visit some of the places he felt he already knew.

As he got off the plane and was processed through Customs, he felt his New York experience had begun early; the woman who was keeping the queue in order and shepherding people to each desk as it became vacant had a strong Brooklyn accent. He was nervous when it was his turn to approach the desk – the US was renowned for tight security even then, and he had a bag full of drugs and sharps but thanks to the excellent advocacy work conducted by both national and international diabetes groups, he cruised through and wasn't stopped, questioned or made to feel unwelcome or nervous.

Once he'd travelled into the city and booked into his hotel – a lovely place not far from the Empire State Building – he checked his itinerary. As well as the Twin Towers and the Empire State Building itself, he planned to take a ferry from Battery Park past the Statue of Liberty and to Ellis Island, where hopeful immigrants had made their first stop in years past. But first, he had some other places to visit, starting with the Waldorf Astoria Hotel, which he knew from Coming to America; the New York library, from Ghostbusters; and then Central Park, from – among other movies – Elf. Next up was Monk's Café from Seinfeld actually Tom's Restaurant on the corner of West 112th Street and Broadway, the inside of which is nothing like its on-screen depiction – after which he got the subway to Central Park West to check out Strawberry Fields, the John Lennon tribute, then have a few beers at the WWF Times Square café.

New York was non-stop but over too soon; despite having packed as much as possible into his time there, many things remained unseen. They'd be top of the list for his next visit, should he get the chance to come back.

His next stop was a welcome return to Paris, somewhere he felt immediately at home. Shortly after he arrived, he checked his diabetes supplies to see how things were going and was alarmed to find that if he kept using test strips at the same rate as he had been, he would run out before he embarked on his planned trek through the Himalayas. The thought of being unable to check his blood sugar in that environment was unthinkable, and while he could say 'I am a diabetic' in many languages, he hadn't thought to learn how to say 'Could I please have some diabetes test strips?' There was only one thing to do; he was going to have to go without test strips for a couple of weeks prior to his trek. He'd done it before when he was at home, it'd be fine!

From Paris, Barnaby headed to Barcelona for a week, and he figured he'd make that the first of his two without test strips. The city was a revelation; it moved to the beat of its own drum. Mornings and afternoons were the same as everywhere else, but lunchtime heralded siesta and the whole place shut down, which took a bit of getting used to. The evenings were different again as everyone, locals and tourists alike, came together to drink, dance and sing Ricky Martin songs. It was quite an experience.

As Barnaby left Spain and headed back to France for a brief stop in Nice, he reflected that he was as happy not to have known what his blood sugar levels might have been while he was in Barcelona; sometimes ignorance truly was bliss!

From Nice, he quickly moved on to Switzerland, and from there took a train to Vienna in Austria, which was where he was to pick up his flight to Nepal.

When he got to his hotel in Kathmandu, he finally opened a pack of test strips. He was nervous as he checked his blood sugar level, but to his immense relief it came out at 5.6.

Reassured that all was well, he checked his kit for the sixteen day long Annapurna Sanctuary Trek, which he would be embarking on in a few days' time.

On the morning of his departure from Kathmandu, he packed and headed to the airport for the flight to Pokhara. The sights as the plane soared and banked, affording fantastic views of the Himalayas, were truly breathtaking.

The trek itself was something Barnaby knew would be as challenging from the point of view of managing his diabetes as it would physically. Exercise and diabetes is something of a balancing act and while he'd got the hang of it as far as football was concerned, a trek meant more sustained activity and he wasn't sure exactly how much extra food he'd need to eat or insulin he'd need to take.

That's why the test strips were so essential.

As it was, he had fast acting sugar tablets for those times he over-estimated his insulin needs or under-estimated how much he should eat.

The trek was an amazing experience; he passed through Gurung villages dotted among the rhododendron forests, then followed the Modi Khola river through the Sanctuary gates and into a hidden amphitheatre, a glacial basin surrounded by the Annapurna massif. It was a spectacular sight, well worth the effort needed to get there and see it.

Back in Kathmandu, Barnaby did some shopping at the markets before hopping on a plane to Sydney.

When he touched down in his home city he felt even more alive after his trip than he had after his tour of Europe. He had seen some amazing sights and met some amazing people; and he'd made some firm decisions about his future, too.

It was March 2000 and Barnaby packed up his life in Sydney and moved to Melbourne, where the Melbourne Demons AFL side had accepted him for pre-season training.

CHAPTER 5:
Another crack at the AFL

There has been rivalry between Sydney and Melbourne for the best part of two hundred years, ever since the colonial government in Sydney imposed punitive restrictions on the settlers of Melbourne. There are pros and cons for each city – provided you aren't a die-hard fan of one or the other – and both regularly appear in lists of the world's top ten best cities in which to live. While Sydney has Russell Crowe, Melbourne has Shane Warne. While Melbourne has less traffic congestion and cheaper housing, Sydney has its beaches and enviable weather. While Sydney has the Opera House, Melbourne has the MCG. Melbourne is also arguably the better of the two cities for fans and players of AFL footy, too.

When Barnaby arrived for his first day of pre-season training with the Melbourne Demons, he was confident, determined and hopeful of ultimately being signed.

Having just travelled around the world, having faced many new challenges and overcome them, whether coping with his diabetes as he journeyed or trekking in Nepal, he felt he could achieve anything.

'So you reckon they'll sign you at the end of pre-season training?' Ashley had asked before he left his parents' home in Sydney.

'Well, I can't know for certain, it's up to the coaches. It's not just a case of being good enough, it's being better than enough other people to qualify for a place.

There are always more athletes than openings.'

'Yeah, but with the Swans, you were one of nine out of thirty who got a place, weren't you?'

Barnaby nodded. 'That's right, I was. I tell you what, though; if I don't get signed it won't be for the want of trying, Ashley. I'm going to give it one hundred per cent, every single day I'm there.'

And Barnaby was utterly determined to do just that; he knew this was to be his final attempt to break into AFL and he intended to give it his absolute best.

He soon fell into a routine training with the Demons and was reminded once again that for him, a career as a professional sportsman was the best job in the world. In almost three months, while pre-season training lasted, he was not once asked to sit at a desk or turn on a computer. No one expected him to wear a suit or have a telephone glued to his ear eight hours a day. Best of all, the only time they were indoors was for weights training.

The conviction that playing in the AFL was his dream job drove Barnaby on: he was determined, focused, and relentless in his pursuit of excellence. When it came to the end of year break, he was on top of the world. Coming second only to former Brownlow medallist Shane Woewoedin in a pre-Christmas skills test was the icing on the cake.

He headed back to Sydney to spend Christmas and New Year with his family and had a lovely, relaxing break. The weather was so much better in Sydney and being with his folks was like a shot in the arm; he felt invigorated when he went back to Melbourne in the New Year.

It was decision time at the club and while time spent waiting to hear was as hard as ever, Barnaby was highly optimistic of being signed – and he was signed, but not by the Demons. He was approached instead by Melbourne's sister club, Sandringham, and offered a two-year contract with them, which he accepted. Sandringham Football Club plays in the league below AFL, so while he wasn't exactly where he wanted to be, he was getting paid to play football. He was also hopeful that if he played well enough, he'd be noticed and might get into AFL via the back door. He continued to give everything one hundred per cent.

It turned out he wasn't the only person from Sydney who was playing for Sandringham in Melbourne and while he made many friends there, he forged particularly strong links with fellow Sydneysiders Richo and Maxy. They trained together and spurred each other on, and socialised together, too. The three of them, plus Patty, Lynchy, Gaddo, Pez, Aines and Troll, often took a footy to the park and kicked it around in their spare time.

As well as footy in the park, for the two years he played with Sandringham he did extra gym sessions and stayed behind at the oval after training to do sprints on his own in the dark. That took his thoughts back to an earlier time, when he'd walked out into the middle of the pitch at Sydney Cricket Ground and had plucked some tufts of grass from the field and tucked them into his wallet. It felt like a lifetime ago; so much had changed, and yet his love of and commitment to the sport had remained constant.

Frustratingly, Barnaby's commitment to training didn't translate into scintillating form during matches and so didn't result in any interest from AFL clubs. When his two year contract with Sandringham was up, he made the decision to head back to Sydney.

'That's rotten luck, you must be really disappointed you didn't get into an AFL club,' Ashley said as they sat in the sunshine, each clutching a soft drink.

'Funnily enough, I'm not,' he replied.

'How come? Did you get sick of being away in Melbourne?'

'No, it's not that.' He took a sip of his drink. 'You see, I knew what I wanted and I went after it wholeheartedly. I couldn't have done any more than I did, I gave one hundred per cent.' And it was true; he felt better about failing with Sandringham than he had about failing with the Sydney Swans, because this time he'd tried his absolute hardest, whereas earlier he knew in his heart of hearts that he could have done more.

'What'll you do now?'

'Enjoy the weather after Melbourne.' 'No, seriously,' said Ashley.

'I'm not sure yet,' said Barnaby. 'I want to check some stuff out before I make a definite decision.'

CHAPTER 6:
Life after footy

What Barnaby did next surprised a lot of people; he signed up for a journalism course at UTS, the University of Technology in Sydney.

'You're going back to school?' said Ashley, grinning, when he told her.

'Not school; university. Just because I can't play footy professionally doesn't mean I'm going to sit behind a desk for the rest of my days; I want to do something more interesting with my life and to do that, I need to learn some new skills.'

'Fair enough, if you put it like that, it makes sense.'

'It's all about having a goal and working steadily towards it at all times.' Ashley nodded; that was something she was getting used to hearing from Barnaby; have a goal, keep moving towards it, always give it one hundred per cent. He was inspirational in that respect and she had learned a lot from him and how he lived his life. He was having a big influence on her outlook, too.

Barnaby's current goal was born out of a chance discovery. While he was in Melbourne, he had come across a diabetes related statistic that told him that diabetes rates among tribal Africans were nearly four per cent lower than for those who lived in cities, and he thought that would be an interesting subject to pursue. What is it, he wondered, that they're doing that's having such a beneficial effect? Whatever their

45

secret was, it deserved to be shared with the rest of the world; it could have a massive impact on people's lives. He was confident it would make a tremendous documentary; he just needed to learn the necessary skills so that he could make it.

There was a slight hiccup when it turned out that documentary production was not a subject offered as an element of the journalism course he was pursuing.

'But I especially want to study it,' he said to the admissions tutor. 'In fact, that's the main reason I'm here.'

The tutor shrugged. 'I'm sorry, it's just not a part of that course.'

'Oh, come on,' said Barnaby, 'there must be something we can do about it. This is important to me; it's not just a whim, I'm doing this degree with a specific goal in mind.'

That caught the tutor's attention. 'Tell me about your goal,' he said.

Barnaby told him what he'd learned about African tribal people and diabetes. 'Diabetes is a disease that affects so many people, myself included,' he said in conclusion, 'that four per cent is a significant statistic. For some people, their diagnosis means the end of their ambition, they think it's a death sentence, but it doesn't have to be like that. I reckon anything that can be done to raise awareness of the disease and, more importantly, to reduce the number of sufferers, has to be worthwhile.'

'You have diabetes?'

'Yes, I was diagnosed when I was fourteen.'

'That must have been rough. Wait a minute, didn't you say you'd also played professional football and travelled around the world?'

Barnaby nodded. 'Yes,' he said, 'but I was lucky. I had a lot of help and support and I was determined it wouldn't beat me. Not everyone is so fortunate.'

'Okay,' said the tutor, 'you're clearly committed to this, so here's what you need to do. If you apply for a special exemption, you should be able to add the documentary production module to your course. There's no guarantee, but it's worth a try.'

'Right,' said Barnaby, 'who do I see about doing that, then?'

By the time term started, documentary production was on the menu; Barnaby's exemption had been granted.

UTS, situated in central Sydney, is one of the biggest universities in Australia and a leading university of technology. Courses include a lot of hands-on, practical experience, and Barnaby felt he was learning real-world skills that would help him both achieve his ambition with regard to the documentary he intended to make and also establish a fulfilling, worthwhile career.

He'd been concerned that he'd be the oldest one there, but not everyone on the course had gone there straight from school. Campus life was vibrant and stimulating, different to anything he had experienced before, and Barnaby made the most of it and also made new friends from amongst his fellow students.

As well as having fun, he approached his studies with the same attitude and dedication with which he had approached sport, and he thoroughly enjoyed the course. In June 2005 he was just one subject away from graduating; that subject, ironically enough, being the one he was most looking forward to: documentary production.

Needless to say, football was still a big part of his life and while he was studying he was also playing footy – and captaining – both the Pennant Hills Demons club side and the Sydney AFL Rep side, a team made up from club side players. Pennant Hills were enjoying a so far undefeated season and just the previous Saturday he'd captained Sydney AFL representative team to victory over the Riverina representative team.

When Barnaby headed out for Thursday night footy practice, he was in good spirits. Since moving back to Sydney from Melbourne he was back in touch with his old friends and he had a bunch of new friends he'd made at university. He was enjoying sport, his studies were going well, and he was already researching the realities of a trip to Africa to make his diabetes documentary. There was just so much to look forward to. Sure, the fight the previous week had been a low point, but there'd been no harm done.

Then it all went pear shaped.

CHAPTER 7:
The rain starts falling:
a stroke at twenty-five

'Where am I?' Barnaby asked. Something was wrong; his voice sounded odd and his face felt stiff. He was hooked up to various machines and monitors and there was a needle in the back of his hand that led, via a length of plastic tubing, to a drip on a stand by the bed.

'Nurse! He's awake!' shouted Ross.

'Oh, thank God,' said Denise, then to Barnaby, 'You had us really scared for a while there, son. I'm so glad to see you again.'

'What happened?'

'You collapsed after training,' said Adam, but before he could say any more, a doctor rushed over to carry out some tests.

'Well, it's nice to finally get to talk to you, Barnaby,' the doctor said. 'Now, how many fingers am I holding up?'

'I'm not sure … two?' said Barnaby.

'That's right.' He held up his pen. 'Can you tell me what this is?' Barnaby squinted. 'Yes, it's a pen.'

The doctor nodded and put it away. 'How's your vision?' 'Not great. I'm seeing double.'

'We'll check that out for you; try not to worry.'

'Doc, what happened? How did I end up here? Have I been here long?'

The doctor was making notes on a chart. 'One question at a time, Barnaby, please. I'll start with the last one first; you've been here in ICU for four days.'

'Four days! You mean it's …' he had to think for a moment, 'Monday?'

'That's right. We've been really worried about you. Your folks have been here round the clock.'

'The last thing I remember is being in the pub for team selections after training. I was named at ruck rover for Penno.'

'You collapsed. Barnaby, you had a stroke, then you went into a coma.'

'What? I thought only old people had strokes.'

'People of all ages have them.'

'What caused it?'

'We'll go into all the details in a little while. The next thing we need to do is a swallow test.' A nurse had poured some water into a plastic cup and she passed it to the doctor. 'Here,' he said, holding it for Barnaby, 'take just a sip.'

Barnaby did, and the doctor watched closely as he swallowed. 'Looks like that went down the right way. That's good, well done.'

'Yeah, it did. Can I have some more now, please? I feel parched.'

'Yes, but don't gulp it. Take it slowly.'

***

'Mum, Dad, it's good to see you.'

'Believe me, it's good to see you, too, Barnaby. We thought …'

50

'We feared the worst,' said Ross. 'We rushed you here on Thursday night and you've been on life support ever since.'

'What happened? I remember training, then going to the pub for team selections and being named at ruck rover for Penno. After that it's a blank.'

'You started seeing double in the pub, so you rang me and asked me to pick you up,' said Ross. 'I did, and when I got you home you passed out at the front door.'

'Really? I just don't remember.'

'You scared the life out of us. We thought it was your blood sugar when you said you were seeing double. Do you remember that was one of the first symptoms you had from your diabetes?' Barnaby nodded. 'Mum and I got you back in the car and brought you straight here to the hospital.'

'I think your dad broke the land-speed record,' said Denise. 'That's when we found out you'd had a stroke.'

Denise was about to tell him that the family had all gathered around his bed ready to say their final goodbyes, that they'd faced the horrific prospect of having to make the decision to turn off his life support, but decided that now was not the time. No doubt he'd get to know eventually, but it was something only to be faced when he was stronger.

Next day, Barnaby saw a neurologist and he explained what had happened. 'When you were attacked when you were out with your friends, an artery near your brain stem was torn. Chance in a million, just really bad luck.' 'And that caused the stroke?'

'You know when you have an old garden hose, there's going to be some build up of gunk in it?'

'I guess.'

'And if it gets bashed, the gunk comes loose and you see it spray out with the water?'

'Yes.'

'Well, after your artery was damaged, it bled and then some of the blood clotted and dried. The dried blood was the gunk that was floating around in your blood stream. While you were training, some of the dried blood got wedged in the torn artery and that meant the blood flow to your brain was interrupted. That caused a stroke and you went out like a light. You were in a coma for four days. We didn't know whether you'd pull through.'

'Maybe it's because my fitness levels are so high.'

'Well, that would certainly have done no harm,' conceded the neurologist.

'I reckon I owe my survival to diabetes,' Barnaby confided in his parents later that day. 'If I hadn't taken such good care of myself and been so fit, it might have tipped the scales the other way.'

'So you think your diabetes might have been a blessing in disguise?' said Denise.

'Like Adam says, sometimes shit just works out.'

'What did you have for dinner?' Denise asked as she sorted through Barnaby's locker. She collected his washing and put his clean laundry in the cupboard and drawers.

Barnaby was struggling to answer the question; he could picture his dinner, but he was struggling to remember what it was called. It was a bird … he just wasn't sure which one. 'Roast pelican,' he said eventually.

'Roast pelican? They're getting more adventurous with their menus since I was last in here,' Denise said. She put some fruit in the bowl on the windowsill then sat down.

'Chicken. I meant chicken.'

'That sounds more like it. Now, how's your physio going?'

***

When the doctor came round next day, Barnaby mentioned to him the problem he was having with words. 'Doc, I keep getting things mixed up,' he said,

'Sometimes I can't even remember what things are.'

'Try not to worry,' the doctor said, 'it's all connected with what's happened to you. Sometimes you'll get a word close to the one you're trying for, sometimes it won't be there at all for a while.'

'Yesterday I told Mum I had pelican for dinner instead of chicken. That's not exactly what you could call close!'

'It is as far as your brain's concerned; they're both birds, after all.'

'I suppose,' said Barnaby, but he wasn't really convinced. 'It will get better though, won't it?'

'It should, and we've got some exercises that will help. It's early days, though, Barnaby. Give it time. You're going to have to learn to be patient and to take things one step at a time. Try not to get too frustrated and if you can't remember something, think about something else for a while and see if that allows it to pop into your head.'

Barnaby nodded. He realised he had no choice; what had happened had been out of his control, and the only way to move forward was to take baby steps.

'Little by little,' he said.

'That's it exactly,' said the doctor.

CHAPTER 8:
Is a 'normal' life good enough?

'Right, Barnaby, let's try to get you on your feet and see how you cope.' Nathan, the physiotherapist flipped the sheets out of the way and helped Barnaby to sit on the edge of the bed. 'Once we've done this assessment, I'll pull a plan together for you and we'll start work on improving your mobility.'

'Great,' said Barnaby. 'I hate the amount of time I spend just lying in bed, I want to start getting back to normal.'

'That's fair enough, but bear in mind you might have to redefine "normal", at least in the short term.' Nathan stood in front of Barnaby. 'Give me your hands and I'll pull you up on three. One, two, three!'

The physiotherapist took the strain and Barnaby was hauled to his feet. 'How does that feel?' he said.

'Weird,' said Barnaby. He didn't feel very secure, even holding on to the physio for support.

'Just stand still for a moment. Don't try to move; aside from anything else, you might get dizzy and I don't want you to fall.'

They stood until Nathan was confident Barnaby seemed steady, then he said, 'Right, I'm going to let go of you now to see if you can stand on your own.' He let go first with one hand and then with the other. For a second, Barnaby stood straight, but then he wobbled and began to topple over.

Nathan caught him as he fell and guided him back on to the bed, where he sat down with a thump.

'Right, that's a lesson learned. We'll get you sorted out with a wheelchair and a walking belt.' Nathan picked up his clipboard and made a note on Barnaby's case notes. 'We'll get you mobile again in time, but for now you're in a wheelchair.'

'A wheelchair! I'm not a bloody invalid!'

'I'm sorry, mate, but for now that's exactly what you are.'

Later Barnaby took stock of his situation. The whole left side of his body had been affected by the stroke; things just didn't work like they used to. It was bad enough that he couldn't walk, but as he and Nathan had established earlier, he couldn't even stand up unaided. For an athlete who loved to be outdoors, not stuck inside, things looked bleak. His footy career was over, that was for certain.

He couldn't brush his teeth, shave, shower, hold a pen or pick up a glass. Then there was his eyesight. Before the stroke it had been fine, but now he needed glasses – although, thank goodness, the double vision had finally subsided. That had been horrible, just a constant headache and a feeling of disorientation.

He sighed. There was nothing to be gained from fretting about things, so he decided to settle down for the night; he could start again tomorrow, keep up with the physio, hope that little by little things would come right. He reached for his glasses with his left hand, intending to take them off and put them on the bedside cabinet, but his arm wouldn't do what he wanted it to. He gave up trying and used his right hand instead, then swore softly under his breath when he realised he couldn't turn over without help. It was going to be a long road to recovery.

Nathan was as good as his word and Barnaby soon had his wheelchair and his walking belt. He was learning to walk again, to keep his balance, to climb stairs, all with Nathan's help. If there was something to hang on to, he could haul himself up from a sitting position with his right hand. He read a little every day, getting used to wearing glasses, taking it slow so he could be sure he'd read what was there and not get his words mixed up. He talked to anyone who came near, thinking that the more words he could say on a daily basis, the more they'd be reinstated in his brain.

He did puzzles: crosswords, acrostics, word searches, Sudoku, anything he could get his hands on, and slowly learned to use a pen again. He took slow, tentative steps, stood up, sat down, stretched, anything that would help his mobility. He didn't mind how difficult it was, he just focused on the task he was occupied with at any one time and gave it his best.

'How do you feel?' Ross asked him on one of his regular visits. Just as he had when Barnaby was hospitalised with diabetes, he'd got into the habit of popping in to see him on his way home from the office.

'Okay, I suppose. I'm improving. It's at a glacial pace, admittedly, but some things seem to be getting a little easier.'

'That's good, but it's not what I meant. How do you feel about the stroke? You've had a bit of time to process it all now. So how are you in yourself?'

Barnaby scratched his head. 'I feel frustrated, mostly. It's the practical stuff, Dad. I can't stand up on my own without falling over, I can't open a door, and I can't even manage to take a drink from a glass of water without help. That should all get better, but it'll take time.' And meanwhile, he thought to himself, I still haven't finished my studies, I haven't got a job and my driving licence has been rescinded because of the stroke. Oh – and I'm still diabetic!

'Are you starting to come to terms with it?'

'I think so. I try not to get too hung up on the big picture, it's overwhelming if I do that. I just focus on the task in hand, whatever that might be, give it one hundred per cent and believe the result will fall my way.'

'That sounds like your approach to everything,' Ross said. 'Well done, son; I have every confidence you'll get through this and come out the other side smiling.'

'I hope so, Dad. Believe me, I'm trying my best.'

In his darker moments, Barnaby had his doubts. He'd seen other people overcome adversity and reckoned they seemed to have superhuman strength, endurance and dedication, but despite having overcome the potential limitations of diabetes, he wasn't sure he had that. His situation alarmed him, but he stopped short of panic because he wouldn't allow himself to dwell on things. He took it one step at a time. 'Focus on the game plan and the result will take care of itself,' he muttered. It had become his mantra.

After a couple of months, Barnaby was discharged and allowed to go home. By the time Ross and Denise arrived to collect him, he'd been sitting with his things packed, ready to go, for a couple of hours. Although his parents pushed him to the car in his wheelchair, he took the walking belt with him; he accepted he needed both the chair and the belt for now, but he was determined to walk again unaided.

Back home, everything looked normal, everything was where it was meant to be, but he was going to have to navigate his way around the place a lot differently now. He had already done a great deal of hard work, much of it painful, and he had a great deal more ahead of him, but he reckoned with guts, graft and a little bit of luck he could beat most of the effects of the stroke. He could already open and close his left hand, stand up without the walking belt and – finally – put his own socks on, and he was convinced his memory had improved.

He might have been improving little by little, but Barnaby became frustrated with the number of different therapists he was seeing. Nothing seemed to quite join up, nobody was looking at the big picture, and he felt that if he were going to make the most of the time and effort that was going into his rehabilitation, he needed someone who could take a step back and make sure he was doing everything necessary.

Greg Castle had been his physiotherapist when he played football and they'd always got on well. He had a lot of respect for Greg, his approach and his skills; he got results. It had been on his mind for some time and by the time he finished outpatient therapy at the rehab centre, he had a plan in mind; he asked Greg to work with him while he continued to recover.

The arrangement worked out really well, Greg knew what he was doing and Barnaby trusted him completely, so he decided to take it a step further by asking him to become his case manager.

'Case manager?' Greg said when he broached the subject. 'What'll that involve, exactly?'

'Pretty much what we're doing now, I guess, plus overseeing all my rehab. Pulling it together, you know?'

'Project managing putting you back together, you mean?' Greg grinned.

'Yeah, I suppose so. Just making sure I do everything I need to and keeping a check on my progress. Stepping it up if I start going backwards, easing off if it gets too much. Understanding what all the various treatments and therapies are all about. Just a joined up approach.'

'Sounds good, mate. Count me in.'

Barnaby had appointments with Greg five days a week, Monday to Friday, and he made steady progress. Some of his rehab exercises were more fun than others: he enjoyed Jenga, Sudoku and Rummikub more than trying to pick a single paperclip out from a bunch in a mug and place it on a dish in his left hand.

Some, like doing cross stitch embroidery, were things he'd never imagined in a million years he would do, but once he was convinced of the benefits, he learned to do it and even enjoyed it.

'Here,' said Greg one day, 'here's something new for you to try.' He handed Barnaby a small oblong box.

'What is it?' Barnaby asked, taking it from him.

'Have a look.'

Barnaby opened the box and looked inside. 'What is it?' he repeated.'

'What does it look like?'

'A load of balls.'

Greg laughed. 'They're Bao-ding balls. Chinese meditation balls.'

'What do I do with them?'

'Here, I'll show you.' Greg took them and showed Barnaby how to rotate the two balls in one hand. 'That's how you use them. See? They're great for improving manual dexterity and strength, so use them in your left hand, okay, mate?' Barnaby took them and tried to move them as he'd seen Greg do, but he fumbled the movement and the balls dropped to the floor and rolled away.

'Shit!' he exclaimed. 'Damn stupid balls!'

Greg stooped to pick them up. 'They're also great for reducing stress,' he said wryly, as he handed them back.

'Yeah? Very funny!'

Barnaby made steady progress, although one of the last things he mastered was to lift his left hand to shoulder level. Once he'd managed to regain his mobility, he had to struggle to exercise full control; his hand was shaky as it moved and for weeks he spilled more soup than he ate from the spoon.

'I'm going in to town to pick a book up,' Ross said to him one day, 'do you want to come?'

'Sure, it'll be nice to get out,' said Barnaby. He put down the meditation balls and hauled himself to his feet.

'You're getting really good with those,' said Ross as he went to get Barnaby's wheelchair.

'It's all the practise,' he said, then added, 'don't bother with the chair, Dad. I want to try to manage without it.'

He put on the walking belt, fastening it round his waist with the velcro straps. 'Just grab me if I wobble, okay?'

'Okay, if you're sure you're ready.'

'I am. I want to try, anyway, and this trip seems like the ideal opportunity.'

They got to the car without incident and Barnaby managed to get into the passenger seat on his own. He hauled himself out at the other end and took slow, deliberate steps along the pavement to the bookshop. As they browsed the shelves, Ross only once had to grab a handle on the belt to steady him.

Back home afterwards, Barnaby poured himself a glass of Diet Coke and sat at the table with it.

'You're doing really well, son,' said Ross, as Barnaby carefully lifted the glass to his mouth and took a drink. 'You couldn't do that a few weeks ago.'

'I know. It seems as though it's all starting to pay off, finally. All those exercises and games and things … they work.'

Within a few more weeks, Barnaby was much steadier on his feet. He started walking whenever he could, and within another month was working on his strength, stamina and fitness levels, including doing hill sprints with Richo, a mate from his days in Melbourne.

'You're doing great, mate,' Richo said as they took a break from their exertions. Barnaby unscrewed the cap from a bottle of water and took a drink, grateful to be able to do such small things again, things he had once taken for granted.

'Yeah, things are getting better,' he said. He put the top back on the bottle. 'One more, then quit?' said Richo.

'Sure, let's go.' As he powered up the hill, Barnaby marvelled at what had happened; he had gone from the peak of fitness to having to learn to walk again, indeed, wondering if he would even be able to walk again, and now here he was sprinting up a hill. It wasn't quite like the old days, but he was getting closer to how he had been before the stroke and he was grateful for that.

***

'What's that you've got there?' Denise asked, seeing Barnaby filling in a form.

'I'm applying to take my driving exam again,' said Barnaby. His licence had been revoked as soon as he suffered the stroke and he was now considered sufficiently physically improved to drive again, although it meant retaking the test.

'Does Greg know?'

Barnaby grinned. 'It was Greg's idea, he's been pushing me to get back to normal.' Barnaby had been out driving with Greg regularly, getting some practise in, getting his confidence back, and they both felt he was ready.

'He's been a real help, hasn't he?'

'Oh, yeah; he got me back on my feet and I reckon with his help I'll soon be back behind the wheel, as well.'

Denise patted him on the shoulder. 'Good for you. I'm proud of you, proud of the way you've handled this whole episode. There's plenty people would have just given in, but not you.'

Barnaby shrugged. 'I guess I learned a lot when I was diagnosed a diabetic.' He thought of Jordan and his mum, how they'd just given up when they got the diagnosis. There was no way he'd ever be like that. He hoped he'd have enough good sense and judgement not to have unrealistic expectations and to know when to give something up as a bad job, but he'd always try to be the best he could be.

On the day of the test, Greg came to pick Barnaby up to drive him to the centre. 'Are you ready?' he asked as they walked into the test centre.

Barnaby nodded. 'As I'll ever be. I just hope I pass.'

He heard Greg say, 'Good luck, mate,' as his name was called and he headed off with the examiner.

Just over an hour later, Greg heard the result and handed Barnaby his car keys. 'There you go,' he said, 'drive us back to your place.'

Barnaby took the keys from him and jumped in the driver's seat.

'And well done, mate. Many congratulations!' Greg said as he got into the passenger seat.

'One more hurdle cleared,' said Barnaby, as he turned the key and the engine fired.

'Well?' said Denise when he got home. Barnaby put on a sad expression.

The smile slid from her face. 'Maybe it was a bit too soon; you can always take it again,' she said, looking to Greg.

Greg grinned. 'Take no notice of him, he's having you on.'

She looked back at Barnaby. 'You passed?'

'Yes,' he said, grinning, 'I passed!'

'That's great, well done!'

'I'm in the market for a car now, I can't wait to get back on the road properly.'

CHAPTER 9:
Playing in the puddles

After a solid year of hard work, pain, and dedication, of challenges met head on and overcome, the time finally came when Barnaby felt able to resume his studies.

When he told his parents, Denise asked, 'Are you sure it's not too soon?' Concern was etched on her face.

'I don't think so, Mum,' he said. 'I've given it a lot of thought and I feel ready to do it. I can walk and I've got a lot of my movement and dexterity back, I'm driving again, my memory and cognitive functioning have improved heaps over the last few months and I'm starting to feel a little more like my old self. I just want to try to get my life back to normal. As near to it as I can manage, anyway.'

'Well, okay then, but if it turns out to be too much, you must promise to admit it. There's no shame in failing because you tried to do too much too soon; you can always walk away and give yourself more time to recover.'

'I know and I will, Mum, I promise.' Barnaby shifted in his chair. 'But I'm so close to finishing the course; I've only got one module left to take, then I'm done.'

'Any thoughts as to what you'll do then, son?' Ross asked.

'Not really, Dad. I just want to finish what I started and graduate. I can worry about the future after that.'

Ross nodded. 'That's the best approach, I reckon. One step at a time, eh.'

Barnaby nodded, but he knew what he'd said to his folks wasn't strictly accurate. Oh, it was true enough that he wanted to graduate; huge chunks of his life had been put on hold for the past year and he wanted to start taking steps to get back on track. Finishing his course was the obvious first step. But there was something else, too. All his time in stroke rehabilitation had given him plenty of time to think, and a plan for the future was starting to take shape.

Despite the stroke, the pain and frustration of rehabilitation and recovery and the little triumphs that had marked his slow march back to health, he had never forgotten the diabetes statistic he had come across in Melbourne; four per cent fewer tribal Africans suffered from diabetes than those based in cities. He had held to that and to his conviction that the reasons behind that fact were important and should be investigated and shared with the wider world.

Barnaby planned to finish his studies by taking the one remaining subject: documentary production. Then he planned to go to Africa to make his film about diabetes and how it was the rates were so much lower there.

There was a third consideration, as well, something that was eating away at him more and more now that he was starting to get his strength back. Up until he'd had his stroke, Barnaby had been brimming with self-confidence and his self-esteem was strong and healthy. Things were going well, he had so much to look forward to and life was an adventure, a trip, an absolute joy. The stroke had pulled the rug out from under his feet in the most cruel and brutal way imaginable; he knew it would have been easy just to fall into despair over it, the way he knew some people did when they found out they'd got diabetes, and he reckoned coping with diabetes was a walk in the park compared to the hard road he'd trodden since the stroke. He felt like he'd lost his mojo, but lately he'd developed a part- formed thought, little more than an instinct, really: the belief that if he went to Africa, he would get his mojo back.

If he'd told his parents he planned to travel so far on his own, however, they'd have had a fit. Better to take it little by little. Having had a bump in his car recently when he accidentally rear-ended the vehicle in front, they were watchful anyway, even though the damage had been easily repaired and no one had been injured. Going back to university was an odd experience. His surroundings were familiar and brought with them a rush of bittersweet emotion; the last time he'd been there, he'd enjoyed full health. But while the place and his tutors were familiar, his fellow students were all strangers, his previous classmates having graduated and left the year before.

Getting back into the routine was hard; there were days he just wanted to stay in bed or to bunk off, but as always he had a goal, a plan, and so he worked hard and took each day one at a time.

The documentary making module was, just as the other elements of his course had been, practical and hands-on, and Barnaby was required to make a short documentary film. After much thought, he decided to make skateboarding the focus of his film, and he roped in a couple of friends, AJ and Harley, to help him. He thoroughly enjoyed the whole process, from shooting footage to scripting the voiceover, then editing it all into a coherent piece of work, and he was absolutely thrilled with his final film. Perhaps even more importantly, his work got him a pass, and in 2007 Barnaby graduated from the University of Technology, Sydney, with a diploma in journalism.

It was a proud day for the entire family when Barnaby graduated. As he stood on the stage alongside his peers, dressed in cap and gown, he could see his folks and his siblings in the audience. Denise clutched a hanky and dabbed at her eyes from time to time, and both parents positively glowed with pride. Once again Barnaby had faced a challenge head on and had overcome it. No one would have questioned him had he decided not to go back to college, but as far as he was concerned he'd left something unfinished. There was an outstanding goal to be hit, and he'd accepted the challenge and had fulfilled his ambition.

As for Barnaby, he was now equipped with the skills he needed to shoot his documentary about diabetes in Africa; all that was left was to finalise his plans, secure a funder and then find a broadcaster.

CHAPTER 10:
Finish what you start

'I'm going to finish my book,' Barnaby announced to his folks at dinner one night.

'Book? What book?' asked Denise.

'After I finished my time with the Swans, I started to write a book. I wanted to do something that would help young kids with diabetes, so they could see it didn't have to hold them back, they could still chase their dreams.'

'I remember that,' said Ross. 'How far did you get?'

'Not very, to be honest, but I've got a new perspective on it now.'

'Yes?'

'Yeah. It's not just about diabetes now, there's more to put in it. I'm going to write about my life so far. I think it might help people.'

'In what way?' asked Ross.

'Well, I've coped with a fair old bit during my life, what with managing my diabetes and surviving the stroke, and I've achieved quite a lot, too. I've proved none of it has to hold you back.'

'And you do have a diploma in journalism now,' said Denise; 'it would be a good way to put it to use.'

'How long will this book be?' asked Ross.

Barnaby shrugged. 'Just as long as it needs to be to say what I have to say, I guess. There's no point in rambling on just to fill more pages up with words if it can all be said more concisely.'

'Sounds like a plan. What are you going to call it?'

'I thought *Sugar, Swans and Stereos.* It's alliterative, it should catch people's imagination and it pretty much sums it all up, don't you think?'

'What about Sugar, Swans and Strokes?'

'Nah, definitely *Stereos*; it's quirkier.'

'Well, you know best. When are you going to start?'

'I've got the stuff I wrote last time and I've made some notes to add to it; I thought I'd start writing it tomorrow.'

Ross nodded. 'Good luck with it. Let us know how you get on.'

Next day Barnaby sat down in front of his computer, a couple of pages of notes on the desk beside it. For all he'd thought he was prepared, he just wasn't sure how to begin. 'It was a dark and stormy night'? 'It was the best of times, it was the worst of times'? First lines were important. *Start at the beginning,* he told himself, *and just work through things as they happened. You can change things later if you have to; just make a start!*

Tentatively he tapped out the first words … 'Growing up as a youngster in the small Sydney suburb of Thornleigh, I guess I always had the makings of a diabetic.' And that was it; he was off the starting blocks. Now it was just a case of keeping going until he got to the end.

'How's the book coming along?' Denise asked him later in the week.

'Slowly,' said Barnaby, then he laughed. 'I get fifty words down then delete ten of them.'

'Well, at least it's a net gain,' said Ross.

'Actually, Dad, you can help.'

'Oh? How's that then?'

'Well, the whole family had to cope with my diabetes; everyone made changes when I was diagnosed. I just think it would be really interesting to get your perspective on what it's like to have a diabetic in the family.'

'I was floored when you were diagnosed; it's every parent's nightmare.'

'Do you think you could write about how it felt? I'll give you your own chapter in the book.'

'Oh, I don't know. How many pages are you talking about?'

'As many or as few as you need. If this book's going to help people, it should look at things from different perspectives, though, don't you think? You could write something that would help other parents whose kids are diagnosed.'

'Well, for what it's worth, I think it's a good idea,' said Denise.

'Thanks, Mum. So, Dad, what about it?'

'I'll give it a go. I'm making no promises, mind, let's just see how things go.'

A couple of weeks later, Ross came in to where Barnaby was sitting in front of his computer; he had a can of Diet Coke in one hand and a sheaf of hand-written pages in the other.

'There you go,' he said, handing the can to Barnaby.

'Cheers, Dad.' Barnaby popped the tab and took a drink. 'What's that you've got there?'

Ross looked at the pages, then at Barnaby. 'I don't know if it's any good,' he said, 'but it's my chapter for your book.'

'Oh, fantastic! Thanks, Dad.' He reached out to take the pages; Ross held on to them. 'Give 'em here, then.'

'Ah, okay. Don't be too harsh, though. I'm not a writer.'

As Ross turned to go, Barnaby started to read. And once he'd started, he couldn't stop. The pages were infused with his dad's warmth and wisdom, and gave a great insight into how it felt when you found out your child was ill, how you learned a lot in a short space of time and how the family had pulled together to cope. And when he thought about how that child had been him, it was both humbling and a reason to feel great pride in his parents and his siblings.

Ross was in the kitchen making a sandwich when Barnaby found him; he didn't say anything, he just hugged him.

'What brought that on?' Ross said when Barnaby let him go.

'Just ... thanks, Dad. Thanks for everything.'

'No problem; it's what I'm here for.' He waved the butter knife. 'Get you a sandwich?'

CHAPTER 11:
I guess it rains:
an African documentary

Despite working on the book, Barnaby still hadn't given up on making his documentary. His initial budget put the cost of the film at $100,000; eleven months prior to his departure date, he had the grand total of $200.

'What are you going to do?' Lachlan asked him as the departure date loomed and Barnaby still had no backer, and no broadcaster lined up for the completed documentary.

'What I always do; get the job done,' said Barnaby. He had looked at his costs and worked out that he could do the job on a budget. If he shot the footage on his handycam, he could self-finance the project and bring it in at around $9,000. After all, there wasn't just the film at stake; he planned to make the story of the documentary the final chapter of his book, and then there was the matter of his missing mojo. Whatever happened, he was going to Africa. Reckoning there was no time like the present, he went ahead and booked himself a plane ticket to Botswana.

First stop on his African adventure was the Mokolodi Game Reserve, over twelve acres of land situated in an acacia bushveld valley around fifteen kilometres south of Gaborone. There Barnaby got a taste of the dark continent and all the challenges that it presented everyone, not just a diabetic stroke survivor. He joined a group of tourists that was being shown around by Keiser, a Botswana bushman who worked as a guide on the Reserve.

'Africa is a dangerous place,' Keiser told the group as he led them through the beautiful, unspoilt terrain, much of it the same as it had been for centuries.

Looking around at his surroundings, Barnaby was awe-stricken. For miles, there was nothing but nature, and the sky was vast. This was the sort of place he could feel at home; no desks, no computers, just the great outdoors. He tuned Keiser back in just in time to hear a warning: 'Water especially is unsafe; don't ever go close to the edge of a pool, there might be crocodiles, and if they get you, you are lost.'

After an enjoyable time at the Game Reserve, it was time for Barnaby to go and see about the documentary. He and his driver Obi set out on their journey to Dovedale Village, three hours north of Gaborone. The plan was simple: live in a rural African village and film the people going about their daily lives, then come back and show the rest of the world the secrets they knew that were helping them avoid diabetes. One thing that wasn't simple was actually getting into the village to shoot the footage.

Barnaby had arranged a meeting with the chief, or 'hosi', in order to put his case forward and ask for permission to live in the village while he shot his film.

When he arrived, he found he faced not only the chief, but also the village police force, who said nothing, but eyed him with suspicion.

He spoke only to the chief, who listened intently while he outlined the idea behind the documentary and the requirements of filming it.

'I will have to speak to the smaller chiefs who represent the people. I will put the matter to them this afternoon; they will vote as to whether they will accept you living among them while you make your film,' the chief said when Barnaby had made his case.

'Oh, okay. When will you have an answer for me?' Barnaby asked.

'Return here in the morning; I will tell you then what they say,' said the chief, and then he stood and left the room, flanked by the village policemen.

It was a long, nail-biting wait to hear whether he'd be allowed in, but Barnaby stayed hopeful. After all, why would they object? He'd do no harm and they might all learn something from one another. Next morning when he went to hear the verdict he was a little apprehensive, but still hopeful.

The chief and the police filed in and the chief took his seat.

'I have spoken to the smaller chiefs, as I promised. I'm sorry,' the chief said to Barnaby, 'you are not welcome to join us and to live among us while you make your film.'

'What? Why not?'

'They do not believe your reason for being here, and so they will not admit you to their community.'

'Can I talk to them? If they meet me, I can answer their questions and put their minds at rest.'

'No, I'm sorry, that isn't possible. That is the verdict they have handed down and the decision is final.'

'Surely I get the right to appeal?' said Barnaby.

'I'm sorry, no.' The chief stood. 'Enjoy your stay in Africa,' he said, and then left the room, flanked – as before – by the village policemen, leaving Barnaby open mouthed.

With a flat out refusal and no right of appeal, Barnaby was stumped.

He'd expected to have lots of questions to answer, had thought he might have to negotiate his acceptance into the community, but hadn't ever expected just to hear a flat 'no'. It was a bitter blow; he had travelled all this way to make a film and now he couldn't even get started.

Luckily for Barnaby, as one door closed another one opened. When he told Chris, Sonia and Elana Schoeman, the Afrikaner family who lived on the farm over the road from the tribal village, of the chief's decision, they immediately invited him to stay with them for the remainder of his time in Africa. If making the documentary had been the only reason for going to Africa, the trip might have been a bust, but there was another reason, a very personal reason, and the Schoeman's generosity might yet allow him to realise his ambition and to rediscover his mojo. The Schoemans had moved to Botswana from South Africa some years before, in order to start a hunting business. They had been successful and the farm was filled with souvenirs: mounted antlers and the heads of elk and impala, and rugs made from the skins of zebras and leopards. It was a far more comfortable home than Barnaby would have had if he'd been allowed into the tribal village.

During his time in Botswana, Barnaby went on a hunting expedition on Dovedale Game Reserve with Chris Schoeman, who unsurprisingly was a skilled hunter.

'Be careful,' Chris cautioned Barnaby as they drove out to the spot he had selected for the hunt, 'Africa is a dangerous place.'

'I'm learning that,' Barnaby said, remembering Keiser's warning about the dangers of getting too close to water – probably the most vital element in the country. 'It's beautiful but deadly.'

Chris chuckled. 'I'd say that's a fair description!'

Barnaby thoroughly enjoyed the day – he was outdoors, after all – and he learned to track and stalk impala.

'If you take a shot, aim to kill,' Chris told him as he set his sights on an animal they had followed for several minutes. 'You don't want injured animals crashing through the bush, you want a clean kill.'

'You're joking, aren't you?' he said, as he saw the line of sight Chris was taking between the trees. 'That gap's way too narrow; you've got no chance of hitting it!' Chris said nothing, just took aim, breathed in, then gently squeezed the trigger as he breathed slowly out. There was a sharp crack and then the animal fell to the earth, blood blossoming on its hide.

'Wow, that was amazing!' said Barnaby. 'Those trees are so close together I'm surprised the bullet didn't get wedged between them!'

Chris grinned. 'That was a great shot, even if I do say so myself. Come on, let's go claim our kill.'

Barnaby caught nothing on the hunt, but he didn't mind; just the experience of being there and learning from Chris was enough.

All told, Barnaby spent two weeks on the farm, and he felt he was close to achieving his objective to rediscover his mojo. For him, his mojo was all about self-confidence and self-esteem, and his had taken a severe beating over the past year or so. His supply was normally brimming over, but lately it had been running dry. Graduation had helped a little, as had working on his book, especially reading what his dad had written, but it was too little. Africa was where he'd hoped to get it all back. And he felt he was getting close; after all, he hadn't come to Africa to have a relaxing experience, he had come to challenge himself and to start to change his bad habits, and he honestly felt like he was making inroads into doing that.

One night as he lay in bed, unable to sleep, turning things over and over in his mind, he had an epiphany. He realised that for him up until now his mojo had been related to his physical appearance and mental ability, and he'd been of the mind that it would officially be back when he was once more the person he'd been before the stroke. The problem with that way of thinking was that it was flawed; he would never again be that person. The stroke had remade him into someone else – like an amputee who waits for his legs to grow back, he was currently living in a dreamland.

Barnaby suddenly realised that he'd never get his mojo back by chasing some old version of himself; that was something that he could never be again.

What he had to do instead was embrace his new self; his mojo depended upon his acceptance that things were different, that his reality had undergone a seismic change and he had been forged anew out of the lightning when it struck.

There was no secret recipe, there were no short cuts for moving forward, there was just good old-fashioned hard work. Dealing with adversity could be boring, but it had to be done. You just had to put one foot in front of the other, head down and bum up, and make sure no one knocked you off the path you'd chosen to take.

Once he'd realised and accepted that, he felt that a weight had been lifted and slept better than he had for months. When he finally said goodbye to the Schoemans and headed to the airport on the day he left Africa, it was with a full quota of mojo under his belt.

Back home in Sydney, he was philosophical about the whole experience. 'But you didn't actually make your film; aren't you disappointed?' Ross asked him.

'Yes and no,' Barnaby replied. 'Yes, it's a shame I didn't get to make my diabetes documentary, definitely. But on the other hand, since I was there for a month anyway, I had a much better time staying on the farm than I would have had staying in a hotel. I saw much more of Africa, for a start, and I had some great experiences and made some new friends.'

He laughed. 'Staying there was a damn sight more comfortable than the tribal village would have been, too.'

'Is Africa somewhere you'd like to visit again?' said Denise.

'Absolutely, said Barnaby; true to form, he already had a plan in mind.

As far as his book, *Sugar, Swans and Stereos*, was concerned, he'd now written the chapter detailing his trip to Africa, and while it wasn't the chapter he'd expected to write, it was honest and it was finished. In fact, not just that chapter, but the book itself, was now finished, despite which Barnaby felt there was something lacking. He wanted the first few pages to have more of a punch.

'Why don't you ask someone to write something about you?' Denise suggested.

'That's a good idea,' said Barnaby. 'Any ideas who?'

'You want a name people will recognise. Is there anybody from your time with the Swans who'd do it, do you think?'

'There might well be; good thinking, Mum!'

Barnaby pulled out his phone and scrolled through the numbers as he headed out into the garden.

'Paul? That you? How are you, mate!'

Fifteen minutes later, he strolled back indoors. 'Paul Roos is going to do it; we were at the Swans together and he was premiership coach the year I had my stroke.'

He still felt there was something missing, however, and he tossed various ideas around over the next few days until finally the penny dropped.

It was a book intended to help people, a response to the time four or five years after he'd first been diagnosed that he'd been asked, and had tried to help, a boy who was then the same age Barnaby had been when he found out he was diabetic. The whole thing was inspired by Jordan, and yet he didn't get a mention.

He started writing: 'Jordan is probably twenty-five now'. Then he went on to outline what had happened and to explain how that had led to the book the reader now held in his hand. That was it; it was done.

With the writing finished, Barnaby designed a cover, got prices from local printers, picked one, and had the book printed.

He handed the first copy out of the box to his dad; Ross opened it and read: "'This book is dedicated to everyone who thought it was possible for me to finish it." That should be everyone you know; you always finish what you start. Your determination is one of your greatest strengths.'

***

Africa wasn't the only place Barnaby got to visit; one of his best mates, Andrew, was living in Singapore and he invited Barnaby to come and stay with him and his partner, Charlotte.

Barnaby met up with them again not long after, this time in Majorca for their wedding. The wedding was beautiful, the happy couple surrounded by their family and friends, everyone wishing them well and enjoying the day. Everything felt both wonderful and normal; this is what people do, this is how life is, he thought to himself, and to be able to be here and share this amazing day with my friends is fantastic.

When he got home, he got a call from Greg Castle; he'd arranged a Demons' ski day on his boat at Apple-tree Bay and wanted to know if Barnaby wanted to go. Of course, he said yes.

On the day, Barnaby discovered that Greg had a wakeboard; rather than being towed behind a boat on traditional water skis, wakeboarders use something that looks more like a snowboard, and indeed, the sport grew out of a combination of water skiing, snowboarding and surfing techniques. It looked like tremendous fun.

'You having a go, mate?' Greg asked, and though tempted, Barnaby shook his head.

'Best not,' he said, thinking about his disabilities. One of the effects of the stroke was that the signal telling the muscles attached to the bottom of his eyes how to move had been affected, meaning he had a lot of trouble looking down.

He'd recently had a second rear-end crash in his car and although once again there'd been no one injured and the damage was easily repaired, he suspected the trouble with his eyes might be a contributory factor and that worried him.

'Are you sure?' Greg said, surprised at the refusal.

Barnaby looked out at the water, at the Demon currently on the wakeboard; he looked like he was having a fantastic time and he and his mates were whooping and laughing. He grinned.

'What the hell,' he said, 'let's have a go!'

'That's more like it – come on!'

The first few attempts were comical and Barnaby learned how to sink rather than to ride the wake, but as always he persevered and he got the hang of it pretty soon. It was exhilarating, really good fun.

When it was someone else's turn and he got the chance to talk to Greg again, he said, 'That was ace, I loved it!'

'I thought you would. It's just your sort of thing.' Greg grinned. 'You're getting back to normal, mate, almost like it never happened.'

Barnaby grinned back; he wasn't sure he'd go quite that far, but it was fantastic to do the things other people did; just a normal life, that's all he wanted.

Shortly afterwards he was driving home one night when he saw an old lady using a walking frame a couple of hundred metres ahead of him. He looked again and she'd disappeared!

I must be tired, he thought to himself, I'm imagining things. No sooner had he thought that than the old lady reappeared, and this time she was only about twenty metres in front of the car. Barnaby's heart hammered in his chest as he slammed the brakes on and prayed the car would stop in time; it did, but he missed her by inches.

'Are you alright?' he said, jumping out of the vehicle.

'Yes, I suppose; that was too close for comfort, though. You should pay more attention!' She glared at him then moved off and Barnaby got back into his car and completed the drive home.

That night he thought about what had happened and realised it was most likely connected to the trouble he had with his eyes, the same trouble that had most likely contributed to the two rear-end crashes he'd had earlier. So far no one had been hurt, but he couldn't guarantee that would always be the case. The old lady could so easily have been seriously injured or killed, and he wasn't sure he could have something like that on his conscience.

As always, he took responsibility and faced the situation head on, and so the next day he went to the Roads and Traffic Authority and handed in his driving licence.

CHAPTER 12:
Mount Kilimanjaro:
the metaphoric mountain becomes reality

'Hey, Ashley!' said Barnaby when his sister answered the phone, how do you fancy climbing Mount Kilimanjaro with me?'

'What? Are you serious?'

'Totally! I reckon it'll be fun.'

'I've wanted to do it for years, you know that, but it was just so expensive … when are we going?'

'Next year. Wait a minute … we? You're in?' He grinned, delighted.

'Damn right I'm in! Who else is going?'

'So far you, me and Jason.'

'The three musketeers.'

'Three Stooges, more like. Listen, we'll talk more soon; I just wanted to ask if you were up for it.'

'Okay, just let me have the details when you know more.'

'Will do; bye, Ashley.'

As he put the phone down, Barnaby was excited; he had a new challenge to plan for, something that even four or five years earlier he would never have dreamed was possible: climbing Mount Kilimanjaro with two of his best friends, his sister, Ashley, and his former AFL teammate, Jason … it would be awesome!

The time between initially deciding to go and the date they were to fly out to Tanzania in Africa passed quickly. By the time they set off on their adventure, they were very well prepared; Barnaby had got the necessary medical clearance, everything was booked, their kit had been checked, rechecked and was packed, and they knew more or less what to expect when they got there.

They were met at Arusha airport by group leader Matt Kershaw, who took them to their hotel. All told, there were nineteen people in the group, nineteen people who over the space of a week or so would go from being in most cases total strangers to teammates who could rely on each other for help and support.

At the initial briefing, Matt explained how events would unfold over the next several days.

'First, I hope you've all got your kit with you. It'll be checked by an experienced mountaineer before we leave tomorrow. I can't stress enough the importance of the right kit.

'Secondly, I'm trusting that you've all got whatever medical clearance you might have needed. We're all trained medics and at all times we will know where the nearest medical facilities are, but we rely on you not to take unnecessary risks. We'll be climbing above 2,800 metres and the air gets very thin at that height.

'The next few days are going to be immensely enjoyable, but also immensely challenging; you need to give yourself the best possible chance of going away with a pocket full of fantastic memories.

87

'Now, on to the itinerary. Tomorrow we'll leave here and head to Mount Kilimanjaro National Park. As you know, we're taking the Marangu route; it's the classic route and also the most popular, and you get to sleep in huts rather than under canvas.'

That had been a big consideration for Barnaby; to meet the challenge he needed proper rest; crikey, they all did.

'We'll trek up to Mandara Hut at 2,700 metres,' Matt said, 'which should take about six hours; that's where we'll spend the first night. Next day we head up to Horombu Hut; the trail is slightly steeper and it takes us to 3,720 metres.

'Day three, we'll take a walk to acclimatise ourselves and then rest, prior to our thirty-six hour push to the summit. We'll take that in two stages. Stage one, we'll set off in the morning of day four and trek to Kibo Hut. We should get there about three in the afternoon. We'll eat and nap, then get up in the evening to set off for Gilman's Point.

'We'll be leaving around ten or eleven o'clock, so we'll be climbing by starlight; we'll get to Gilman's point in time for sunrise, then, for those who want to, we'll travel along the rim of the crater to Uhuru Peak; at 5,896 metres, it's the highest point in Africa.'

Barnaby knew the statistics and the itinerary off by heart; he felt that he'd been working towards this trip for six solid years. Kilimanjaro was the reward for all the hard work he'd put in to his rehabilitation, although he wasn't there because he'd had a stroke, he was there to have a holiday with his mates.

When he went to bed that night, he was excited at the prospect of the challenge and, as always, determined to meet it head on.

Next day they were driven to Mount Kilimanjaro National Park for the start of their adventure. They piled out of the bus to the now familiar greeting in Swahili, 'Jambo! Jambo!', as the porters and guides swarmed round to greet them.

Their lead guide, Felix, was highly experienced; he had climbed Kilimanjaro more than three hundred times.

Once they were organised, they set off through the Marangu Gate, the entrance to Mount Kilimanjaro National Park, and as they filed through the gate, they each touched it for luck.

The first day was a relatively easy five hour trek through dense rain forest. As they walked they saw brightly coloured birds flitting between the trees, and spotted various types of monkeys in the branches, their calls and song providing the soundtrack to the journey. The group arrived at Mandara Hut, where they were to spend that night, and got their first look at one of the mountain huts they'd be staying in as they trekked up Kilimanjaro. The huts were wooden dormitories with steeply pitched roofs, but they meant a night sleeping in a bed rather than on the ground. The physical demands of the next few days were going to be high enough without adding to them unnecessarily!

Next day they set out on the six hour trek to Horombu Hut. That stretch of the journey was more demanding, but the stunning scenery certainly helped people along as the dense rainforest yielded to alpine meadow peppered with giant heather trees, the snow-capped peaks of Kibo and Mawenzi visible in the distance.

As Barnaby walked, he had time to reflect. He knew from his research that around twenty-five thousand people a year climbed Kilimanjaro and that, since he was on the most popular of three routes, many feet had trodden the same path his now did and many more would follow him. When they set out, they all wanted to get to the summit, but only around two thirds made it all the way to the top.

That wasn't what mattered, though; Barnaby knew it wasn't the destination, it was the journey that shaped people and made them who and what they were, and he was delighted to be sharing his journey with such very good friends.

Horombu Hut, their next stop, was situated in a rocky valley, and the group arrived there without incident. They were to spend the next two nights there, with just an acclimatisation walk to the saddle of Kilimanjaro on the third day, to allow them to recharge their batteries prior to the push to the summit.

They set out early on day four, walking over open terrain under clear skies.

The air was noticeably thinner and the pace slower, but after seven hours they made it to Kibo Hut. It was time to eat and then grab some sleep, as the next stage of their climb would take them to the summit.

They were awoken at around ten o'clock that night and set off on their journey at eleven, after a refreshing drink of hot tea and singing a good luck song together. Although there was still some light in the sky when they left, that soon bled away to leave a velvet sky studded with bright diamonds. With no artificial light to pollute the skies, the stars were bountiful and bright.

As the group zig-zagged their way up the large scree slope that would take them to Gilman's Point, they were cold, despite their exertions. As they continued to climb the sky began to lighten, heralding the new day, and as they reached the summit dawn broke in spectacular fashion, as the sun burst brilliantly over Mawenzi Peak, bathing the summit and the ice fields in a glorious roseate glow.

'Wow,' said Ashley, 'I have never seen anything so beautiful.'

'It's absolutely stunning,' Barnaby agreed. 'I feel like I'm standing on top of the world.' They stood transfixed while they got their breath back after the long, arduous climb in the thin atmosphere.

'I can't believe you made it, after everything you've been through,' Jason said.

'For sure,' said Barnaby, 'it's been a long journey, in more ways than one.'

Ashley hugged him as he added, 'But you know what? Whoever you are or wherever you come from, the view from the top is the same for everyone.'

The three friends took some time just to appreciate where they were and what they had achieved. Barnaby had been working towards that moment ever since he woke up from his stroke in the ICU. He had loved his life prior to the stroke and had wanted it back if at all possible; standing on the summit of Mount Kilimanjaro, his friends at his side and the spectacular views of the ice fields before him, the vastness of the African plains in the distance, he felt as close to being his old self as he had since he had actually been his old self. It was both humbling and empowering, and he breathed in the moment, taking time to embed the memory in his consciousness; there'd no doubt be times ahead when that memory would sustain him and he wanted to make sure it wouldn't fade.

'Who's coming to Uhuru Peak?' Felix, the guide, asked, once the pyrotechnics of daybreak were over.

'Are you up for it?' Jason asked, and Ashley and Barnaby both nodded.

'Ah, Barnaby, I know you're keen to go,' said Felix, 'but the path to Uhuru is very narrow and slippery, and it's angled towards the volcano crater. I think it will be too dangerous for you. I'm sorry, you need to turn back here.'

'We'll go back with you,' said Ashley. She looked at Jason and he nodded.

'No, no way,' said Barnaby. 'You had your heart set on it. Go, please.' Ashley hesitated.

'Go!'

'Are you sure?'

'Definitely. I'm thrilled to have been able to get this far.'

Barnaby watched as his friends started the two hour trek along the rim of the crater to the very top of Africa. Yes, he would have liked to have been able to accompany them, but he had already, quite literally, climbed a mountain.

For someone who just a few years before had been unable to stand unaided, he was justifiably proud of what he had achieved.

That element of their trip over, the friends went on safari at Tarangire National Park. It was a wonderful experience and with no animals in cages, every sighting was a surprise encounter. At one point a caravan of around fifty migrating elephants passed them by, animals of all ages and temperaments plodding along together, with every now and again one of them raising their trunk to trumpet their presence. A little further along, they saw a committee of vultures feasting and realised they were tearing at the hide and flesh of a dead elephant; seeing such a powerful creature being ripped apart was incongruous, but then that was the cycle of life.

That evening at their hotel a group of local musicians performed for them, a noisy, exuberant show that it was impossible not to get caught up in, then next day they were off to a watering hole for more animal spotting. Out of Africa's 'Big Five' they had so far seen rhinos, elephants, buffalo and lions; only the notoriously difficult to spot leopard had eluded them.

The final part of their trip involved meeting local people and primary schoolchildren, and even teaching some classes. Needless to say Barnaby and Jason teamed up and did their best to get at least the main points of Aussie Rules Football over to them!

Back home in Sydney, Barnaby thought back over his trip and realised that so much of it had been about connecting with other people, understanding them and their situation and making a difference, however small, to their lives.

He'd always remember the people he'd met and connected with in Africa and he reckoned they'd always have their memories of the trip and the connections they'd made, too.

In his life, Barnaby had faced some enormous problems and had overcome them; he'd had some amazing experiences and had learned a huge amount about the world, about other people and about himself. He realised that if he could put that to good use, connect with people and make a difference, then that would be a fantastic path for his life to take.

CHAPTER 13:
The footballer who retired on his own terms

For the previous few years, following his recovery from the worst of the effects of the stroke, Barnaby had once more been part of the Pennant Hills footy club. Okay, so he couldn't play anymore, but he could still be involved, and he was, running water, running messages, doing whatever he could; he just wanted to be close to something that had been such a big part of life for so long. Besides, the guys at Penno were family; he had been just eight years old when his dad first signed him up there to play Aussie rules footy. As far as the game was concerned, though, it was just a spectator sport now, and for the last eight years he had learned to be content to watch from the sidelines.

Barnaby had recently taken the first steps towards establishing a career as a motivational speaker, and now he had an idea. He approached Ian Parker, the vice-president of Pennant Hills. 'Hey, Chicken,' he said, using the VP's nickname, 'you know I've started doing motivational speaking; is there any chance I could do a talk after the game with the Eagles on Saturday?'

'Sure,' came the response, 'I don't see why not.'

And so Barnaby geared up for the talk. It was something he loved doing, a way to help, to give back, and people really did seem to connect with and respond to him, and to get a lot out of it.

Barnaby finished his talk that Saturday to loud applause, and he had the satisfaction of a job well done. He'd connected, there had been a two way vibe, and everyone had enjoyed the experience. There was a further surprise in store, however, as he found out when Chicken walked out in front of everyone. When the applause died down, Chicken said, 'That was great, Barnaby, just fantastic. And do you know what? I'm going to get you back on the ground and you're going to play your hundredth game.'

'What? Are you serious?' Barnaby grinned as the applause from the crowd started up again.

'Absolutely. You'll need to get medical clearance and we'll do everything through all the right channels, but you're going to play your hundredth game for the Demons.'

When Barnaby got home and broke the news to his parents, their responses couldn't have been more different.

'Don't be stupid, you'll get smashed!' said Denise, horrified. 'You can't see well enough … it's dangerous, Barnaby, you could be hurt.'

'Yeah, go to it,' said Ross, 'that'll be awesome.'

Denise shot her husband a look then fixed her eyes on Barnaby. 'You check with the doctor and if he says you can't do it, then you can't; do you hear me, young man?'

Barnaby grinned; it didn't matter what age he was, he was still Denise's son. 'Of course, Mum,' he said, 'I promise.'

Later that week Barnaby got medical clearance and on Thursday night he turned up for practice, just like old times. He fell into the routine as easily as if it had been eight weeks he'd had away from the game, not eight years. He was more cautious than he would have been back then, but that was because he had to test his limits. There was no point in being foolish.

'I didn't realise how much I'd missed it,' he told his parents when he got home from practice, 'I thought it was enough to still be part of the club, but being a player is ... it's a different dynamic to being an official; I really have missed it.'

'You certainly look like you enjoyed it,' said Ross, smiling.

'I'll say! I'm on cloud nine.'

'Footy's a part of who you are,' said Ross.

'For sure; and this has been unfinished business; this is a chance to tie things up.'

Despite his enthusiasm, Barnaby had to work within his limitations. He needed to learn to cope with his co-ordination and spatial awareness, which still caused him problems. One of the toughest things was that despite being a natural left foot kicker, he had to learn to kick with his right due to the effects of the stroke, but he approached it all like everything else; he focused on the game plan.

When he ran out with the team wearing a Pennant Hills jersey for what would be the first of four games (he had played 96 games for the Demons before having his stroke), he was jittery, but his nerves had less to do with any danger or problems his stroke might cause than it did with the eight year break; he didn't want to let his teammates down.

'How did it feel?' Ross asked him when he got home afterwards.

'Oh, it was fantastic, Dad, just fantastic. I mean, I expected to enjoy it, but it was so much more ... I was knocked out by it. The emotion ...'

'Bound to be emotional; you've just done something you never thought you'd do again.'

Barnaby nodded. 'I guess I just wasn't prepared for how much it would all snowball.'

'You enjoy it, son, you deserve this.'

Later that week, after training, one of his teammates, Luke Turner pulled him to one side. 'How's it all coming along, mate? You getting back in to it alright?'

'I love it, it's amazing to be playing again.'

'Any problems?'

Barnaby laughed. 'Loads, but nothing I can't handle.' Luke grinned.

'Seriously, though, there is one thing; without my glasses all I can see is a red blur coming at me when I'm near the footy. I don't know what I can do about that, though; it isn't practical to wear my glasses when I play.'

'True enough; they wouldn't last five minutes.' Luke grabbed his jacket from the peg. 'You coming for a beer?'

That Saturday, Barnaby ran out again with his teammates and again thoroughly enjoyed being back on the field, although the issue with his sight continued to trouble him. *It's just two more games*, he reasoned, *I can cope. I just have to be careful.*

Mid-week training went well; he was getting back into the swing of things and enjoying every moment. Then the following Saturday, when he turned up to prepare for his ninety-ninth game, there was a surprise in store.

'Hey, Barnaby,' said Luke Turner, 'we've got something for you.'

'Yeah? What's that, then?'

Everyone gathered round and Luke handed over a small package. 'Here you go; these should help.'

Barnaby looked at the parcel and wondered what was in it. Everyone was smiling and nudging each other, so whatever it was, they were clearly all in on it. He shook the package, but nothing happened. Intrigued, he tore the paper off.

'Sports glasses!' he exclaimed. 'How did you …'

Luke shrugged. 'You said you were having trouble seeing the ball up close, so me and the guys had a whip round, then I had a word with your folks and we got these made up to your prescription. Go on, try them on.'

Barnaby put the glasses on and tightened the strap; they felt nice and secure and he reckoned they would stay in place no matter what he did on the field.

'That's fantastic, guys, thank you so much,' he said, looking round at his fellow team mates; he was overwhelmed by their kindness and generosity.

'No worries,' said Luke. 'Now, let's get out there and kill them!'

The sports glasses made a tremendous difference to Barnaby's game and he was delighted with his improved vision; he felt the glasses allowed him to make more of a contribution during the game and he loved that. As he ran off the field after the final whistle, he realised he had just one more game to go to meet his goal and he was thrilled at the prospect.

Family and friends flew in from all round the globe for Barnaby's one hundredth game, including Lachlan from Perth and Ashley from London, and the crowd at Ern Holmes Oval broke all records.

'How do you feel?' Adam asked him on the morning of the match.

'Excited; nervous; it's just fantastic,' Barnaby said. 'Bring it on!'

For him, the best bit, as always, was the five minutes before the game in the changing room with the boys, discussing tactics and trying to psych each other up. 'Come on,' said Barnaby as they prepared to leave the changing room for the match, 'let's go and take these blokes apart!'

Barnaby was bursting with pride as he ran out for the last time in the red and blue jersey. As he ran onto the pitch he saw a tunnel formed by other Pennant Hills players, and even the day's opponents, Manly Warringah. He ran through the tunnel, cheers ringing in his ears, and out onto the pitch.

As things got underway, the crowd roared and Barnaby kicked the first goal of the match, from a distance of almost forty metres.

It was a hard-fought game and the scores were tight. With just minutes to go, Pennant Hills earned a free kick and the umpire was persuaded to allow Barnaby to take it.

He agreed, and Barnaby stepped up to take the ball. The tension was palpable, the crowd fell silent, every eye was on him. He took a deep breath to steady himself, ran forward, dropped the ball and swung his right foot to connect, then stared and hoped. As everyone watched, hearts in mouths, the ball soared straight and true.

'GOOOAL!' screamed the crowd, as the umpire blew his whistle and Barnaby was mobbed by his teammates.

'We won!' shouted Chicken, running onto the field, 'and Barnaby scored the first and last goals!' He grabbed the younger man and hugged him. 'Well played, son!' It was a highly emotional moment and Barnaby might have been overwhelmed, had his teammates not grabbed him, lifted him to shoulder height and chaired him from the field, victorious, in a perfect storm of cheers and tears.

His one hundredth game; he could hardly believe he'd done it. The fact that he kicked two goals in his final match was the icing on the cake.

'How do you feel?' a reporter from the local paper shouted to him as he was chaired past.

Barnaby grinned. 'Stick a knife in me, I'm done!" he shouted.

After the match, Barnaby left the changing rooms and jogged over to where his family were standing talking with journalists and Pennant Hills officials.

Adam was saying, 'It's pretty impressive ... given where he has come from was life support, at one stage, then wheelchairs and rehab and learning how to do everything again. People don't know what it takes for him to kick a ball, to drop a ball on his boot and get a handball.'

'Son, there you are!' said Ross. He hugged him. 'I can't believe you did it; I thought your chances of playing footy again were non-existent. Crikey, after the stroke, I wasn't even sure you'd walk again or live a normal life. I'm so proud of you.'

'Thanks, Dad, he said. 'My one hundredth game is probably the most significant thing I've done since having the stroke. I honestly didn't realise it would mean as much as it does. And I can't think of a better way to end my footy career – two goals in my final game after eight years out.'

'You've set such a great example, you've been an inspiration to us after your stroke,' Ross said.

'I don't think Barnaby realises what a contribution he's made to the welfare of this club,' said Peter Campbell, the president of Pennant Hills. 'What happened here wasn't just about one person, it was about bringing the club together.'

Barnaby shrugged. 'I just do what I was told by the coach years ago: I focus on the game plan. I get up every morning and do the best I can.'

'Are you sure you're ready to hang up your boots?' asked Lachlan.

'Yes!' said Denise, emphatically. 'Enough is enough!'

Barnaby laughed. 'Yes,' he said, 'I'm sure. No more AFL, from now on I'm just a normal person again. Which just proves that normal is good enough.'

Later that year, Barnaby was at the Doltone House in Sydney to be inducted into the Sydney AFL

Hall of Fame. He was the second of two inductees and when it was his turn, the guests were first shown a short film that had been on Channel 7's AFL programme, *Game Day*, earlier in the year, then Tom Harley stood up to speak and gave a rundown of Barnaby's achievements:

'Pennant Hills junior under nine to under seventeen; NSW/ACT RAMS team 1996, captain 1997; Ken Macrae shield for best first year player at Pennant Hills in 1996, Pennant Hills best first year player; Sydney Swans rookie list 1998; Rod Podbury medallist as VC victor in 2000; invited to do a pre-season with Melbourne FC AFL 2002; represented New South Wales in National County Championship 2004; Pennant Hills captain 2004/2005; captained Sydney AFL representative team to victory over the Riverina rep team in his last game prior to having the stroke – he collapsed after training the following Thursday. He was also three times runner up in the Phelan Medal, the last time in 2005, and he had the stroke in June of that year.' Tom paused, then said, 'I'd like to announce the second 2013 Hall of Fame inductee, Barnaby Howarth!'

The applause was instantaneous; in seconds everyone was on their feet, clapping, as Barnaby walked up to front of the room. He paused as he put his jacket on, then stepped up to the lectern. Still the applause continued and he smiled while he waited for it to die down. The goodwill in the room was palpable; it was a fantastic experience to be the recipient of so much admiration.

'My best footy coach was a guy from Pennant Hills, Danny Ryan,' he said, as the level of applause dropped slightly. 'And he always said to me "Focus on the game plan and the result will take care of itself". When I had the stroke, that's exactly what I did. Every morning I would wake up and there'd be some new challenge to overcome, so I'd get up and I'd focus on that and overcome that.

'So when Chicken, our vice-president, said, "You can play your hundredth game in fourth grade," I could have pinched myself. I went home and spoke to Mum and Dad and said I'd been offered the chance to play my hundredth game and Mum said, "Don't be stupid, you'll get smashed!" Roscoe said, "Yeah, go to it, that'll be awesome."' He paused as the audience laughed.

'I had no idea it'd mean so much to me. Playing footy in Sydney has meant a lot to me; being involved with the Pennant Hills footy club has meant a lot to me, but if I looked at the big picture of what my life might have been like I just looked at every step along the way, and tonight just completely blows me away.

'That hundredth game was in July and I'm still pinching myself, so to get this is just ridiculous. I almost feel I shouldn't accept it.' He paused. 'Wasn't the criteria that you had to be retired three years? My last game was in July! So thanks, but I don't think I can take it.'

He smiled and the applause started up again as he was presented with his Hall of Fame trophy; and of course he did accept it. It was such a fantastic accolade.

When the presentation was over, Barnaby looked at the crowd as they gave him three cheers, then, his ears ringing, he headed back to his seat, clutching his trophy.

It was one of the proudest moments of his life.

CHAPTER 14:
'Normal' is good enough

'I'm a type one diabetic and a stroke survivor,' said Barnaby. 'I'm also an ex-AFL footballer with the Sydney Swans, an author, a filmmaker, I've climbed Mount Kilimanjaro and I've played one hundred games of AFL with the Pennant Hills Demons.'

Barnaby looked round at his audience as he spoke, taking time to make eye contact with every one of them, just as he'd been in the room to greet each one as they arrived. It was all about connecting with people; that's what made the difference. As he told his story, he could see that people were listening and empathising; they were even laughing at the jokes!

'I want to talk to you today about dealing with disappointment,' he said. 'When we feel like things aren't going our way, it's the decisions we make then that define us. Life isn't fair. But when bad things happen, as they do to all of us, dwelling on the "Why me?" and the "What if?" of a situation is a complete waste of energy. Do you know what I love? I love seeing people who are scared of doing something and who do it anyway. I love seeing people overcome their fears.

'I'll give you a great example of that. In October 2013, I organised an event called "Give it a Crack". It was a night of entertainment put on by performers who had wanted to do something their entire lives, but who had just kept putting it off.'

Barnaby was smiling as he thought about it; people had challenged themselves, had acknowledged the reality of their fears then had faced up to them and done whatever it was anyway. His old Sandringham teammate, Patty, had flown from Melbourne to play a guitar solo. No more 'What if?' Just the feeling of satisfaction you get when you do something you've yearned to do but didn't previously have the guts for.

It was something he understood perfectly; he'd been paralysed with fear himself before and he'd just closed his eyes and jumped in anyway. No one would ever say it was easy, but it beat the hell out of inertia. Nine times out of ten doing something – anything – was better than doing nothing. He seemed to have struck a chord with people, too; 'Give it a Crack' had been a great success and the event was moving up for 2014 from Thornleigh Community Centre to Sydney Comedy Store.

He had come to the end of his talk; it was time to wrap things up.

'I really struggled to find my place in the universe after I had a stroke, but now I know where my place is; it's right here,' he said, pointing to the floor on which he stood. 'Rain falls on the just and the unjust alike. There comes a time when you just have to get over it and go and play in the puddles. Thank you.'

He nodded to his audience and took a step back, and they burst into a round of applause. His career as a motivational speaker was taking off. People liked him, and they seemed to like hearing his stories, too. Chatting to people afterwards he could feel there was a new energy about them, then watching as they left the room he could see there was a spring in their step; he was making a difference.

One of Barnaby's early bookings had been just over a month after he had played his one hundredth game; he was invited to Coolamon golf club by Coolamon RFL club coach Matt Hard to speak to the team players and other members of the community.

When he'd finished speaking, Matt came over with club president Warren McLoughlin, who shook his hand. 'That was fantastic, Barnaby, thank you,' Warren said.

'Thanks. It seemed to go down well, anyway,' Barnaby said, looking round.

'Definitely,' Matt agreed.

'Well,' said Warren, 'I guess when you shove that story in front of blokes it makes them sit up and take notice. I reckon it's good for our guys, not so much their development as footballers, but for their development as blokes.' Barnaby nodded; as well as speaking that night, he was booked to address the players before the next day's game at Kindra Park.

'I just want people to keep moving forwards if they get knocked by disappointment, you know?' he said. 'The tools people need to get on with their lives are right in front of them; they just need to realise it.'

Later that year Barnaby had another wedding to go to, this time in Curitibia, Brazil. One of his old mates from Sandringham, Andrew Treloar – Troll – had gone to Brazil and asked his girlfriend's father – in perfect Portuguese – if he could have his daughter's hand in marriage. To Andrew's immense relief, the answer had been 'Yes' and so he and Flavia were getting married.

Before the day of the wedding itself Barnaby and the other guests were taken to two football matches, one featuring each of Curitibia's teams.

'Who do you support?' he was asked afterwards. 'Which of Curitibia's teams is your favourite?'

'I don't know that I can choose,' he said, 'I like them both.'

'Very diplomatic!' came the reply.

The wedding itself was a lovely occasion; again, friends and family came together to celebrate with the happy couple and everyone had a fantastic time.

After the wedding, Barnaby went with his friend Mark Ainley (Aines, also an old Sandringham team mate), Mark's wife Emily, and Emily's family to visit Iguazu Falls. Situated on the border of Brazil and Argentina, the spectacular Falls – taller than Niagara, and twice as wide – were declared to be one of the New Seven Wonders of Nature in 2011.

They are said to have been created by an angry god when the woman he wanted to marry took flight with her mortal lover. As they sought to escape by canoe, the god divided the river, creating the falls and preventing their escape. The Falls have featured in a number of films, including Indiana Jones and the Kingdom of the Crystal Skull.

Back home, after attending yet another wedding and spending time with other friends who were also married – and starting to have kids now, too – Barnaby wondered if it would ever be his turn.

Was it realistic at thirty-four to expect to find the perfect partner?

Shortly afterwards a mutual friend set up Barnaby and Angela on a blind date. They went to dinner and while he had no prior expectations as to how things might turn out, he found himself in the company of someone he felt immediately at ease with. They talked for hours, it felt like they'd known one another for years.

As they got to know each other better, they discovered that they had many things in common. Unlike in other relationships, where partners made concessions in order to accommodate one another's likes and interests, they both enjoyed the same things. Barnaby took Angela to watch the AFL and Angela took Barnaby to church on Sunday mornings.

Around four months after they first met, Barnaby sat gazing at a sticking plaster on his finger, feeling dazed, not quite sure what had happened.

'Everyone stares at their Band-Aid,' the paramedic who'd put it on told him. 'Patients are always fascinated by it.'

'What happened?' he said.

'We responded to a call from your girlfriend,' he said. 'We checked your blood and you were hypoglycaemic. Your blood sugar was down to 1.9.'

That evening he was talking to Denise on the phone. 'Angela saved my life today,' he said.

'What happened?'

'I misjudged my diabetes management; I had too much insulin and not enough carbohydrate and I slipped into a diabetic coma. Luckily she was there and she didn't panic; she called for help.'

'You were very lucky; how did it happen?'

Barnaby shrugged. 'I guess I just got complacent and I misjudged it. Angela saw that I was non-responsive and she got help.'

'Did you take the day off work to recover?'

'No, I was fine once the paramedics had sorted me out. Angela got me a coffee, and in fact, not only did I get to work on time, thanks to her I was early!'

'Well, take more care, do you hear? Next time you might not be so lucky.'

'I hear you. I certainly don't want to go through that again!'

The incident had really made Barnaby sit up and take notice. He was aware that diabetes couldn't be beaten and that sufferers daren't get sloppy with their control, ever. He'd been living with diabetes for nineteen years and it had still managed to catch him out. He was just grateful that Angela had been there to help him. He was enormously impressed with the way she'd kept a cool head and deeply grateful to her for handling the situation with such aplomb. She really was someone special.

About six weeks later, Barnaby and Angela were sitting on a bench at Bronte beach, enjoying the fresh air and the sunshine.

'Just look at this,' he said, 'it's so beautiful here.'

'For sure. I reckon we're very fortunate to be living in Sydney. We've got the best of everything.'

'No doubt about it,' he said. Life was pretty much perfect; in fact, after finding Angela he reckoned it had been better than perfect.

For a diabetic, however, that can change in an instant. Next day Barnaby almost didn't wake up because his blood sugar level was so low, and once again, it was Angela who saved his life. Realising after what had happened earlier that he was having a hypoglycaemic reaction, she gave him a shot of Glucagon to get his functions back to normal.

'That's twice you've saved my life,' he said. 'Thank you.'

'Thank you' seemed inadequate, but what else could he say? He felt blessed to have such a terrific woman in his life. Not only had she saved his life twice now, she was gorgeous, kind, loved her family, and made tense situations calm.

She really did make the lives of the people around her better.

Barnaby had hoped that would be the last of his diabetes-related mishaps, at least for a while, but in April 2014 he had a nasty moment of déjà vu; he woke up in a Sydney hospital with no idea how he'd got there.

'What happened?' he asked the doctor who was tending to him.

'You were found passed out in the street. The paramedics picked you up and brought you in. Your blood sugar level was dangerously low; you were lucky you were found.'

'No kidding,' said Barnaby. Diabetes was an unforgiving condition.

'What do you remember about it?' said Ross, when they were talking a couple of days later about what had happened.

Barnaby scratched his head. 'Well, I was at work as usual then, when I finished, I got a bus to go to and meet a mate at Bunnings in Randwick, but I ended up in Kingsford.'

'Didn't that tell you something was wrong?'

Barnaby nodded. 'I should have realised then that I wasn't thinking straight and checked my sugars, but instead I got a bus back into town to try again. It was when I got back to town things really turned pear shaped.

'As far as I can tell, I must have wandered around in a stupor until I finally passed out in a lane between George Street and Pitt Street. I reckon I must have lain there on the ground for about two hours until somebody spotted me and called an ambulance. When they turned up, they gave me some glucose and took me to Sydney hospital, where they stabilised me.'

'Barnaby, you've been living with diabetes for years. You've trekked in the Himalayas and climbed Kilimanjaro and coped with conditions there. How did something like this happen here?'

'Simple; I had something different for lunch. I had my regular dose of insulin, then got a crepe. Turned out it didn't have the right amount of carbohydrate to match the insulin I'd had and my blood sugar level dropped too low.' He shrugged. 'That's all it takes.' He paused. 'I guess I was lucky; I made it back home fine and my sugars were back to normal next day.'

'What if it happens again?'

'I've ordered an emergency ID bracelet, so that should help, but that incident showed me that diabetes horror stories aren't confined to young children or the newly diagnosed, they can strike anyone of any age at any time.'

Earlier on the day it had happened, Barnaby had been speaking to a young diabetic girl about telling the story of her struggles with the disorder at a diabetes fundraiser he was MCing in August 2014 to try and raise awareness of the condition and highlight the importance of finding a cure. With diabetes levels rising, he was convinced that was needed more than ever.

'We need a cure,' he said. 'In fact, it's long overdue.'

'Meanwhile?'

'You can't ever BEAT life or adversity, you can only keep moving forwards through it, and you can either move forwards with your head down and your shoulders slumped, or you can go with your head up and your chest out.'

'That's a great philosophy, son. Life according to Barnaby!'

CHAPTER 15:
Life according to Barnaby

When I had my stroke in 2005, I was scared that I didn't have the superhuman strength, endurance and dedication that people who overcome adversity seemed to have. I had a bit of gumption, but I was a university student who played local footy on the weekend – I didn't know if that gave me enough gumption to get me through a stroke recovery.

I got even more worried early in my recovery when I didn't do any of the things I thought people who do something special after disappointment usually do – I didn't have a life changing epiphany, I never looked intensely at myself in the mirror and told myself to 'aim for the moon, 'cause if you miss, you'll still fall amongst the stars', I didn't set myself any lofty goals, make huge sacrifices, and charge towards them hell for leather. Besides a change in my physical appearance, I was still the same bloke – I went back to university and finished my diploma, and my family took me down to the footy in my wheelchair. Nothing had changed – I was still an everyday Joe Sack o' Rolls, and I didn't know if that was enough to give me the life I wanted.

The most passionate feeling I have towards my stroke after nine years of rehabilitation is one of relief. I'm relieved because the gumption I had as an everyday man on the street was more than enough. I was pretty disappointed when I had my stroke, but after going without so many things I'd taken for granted for so long, I have been relieved to find that all you need in life to be happy, is to give one hundred per cent to the task in front of you, and let the chips fall where they may.

Or, as the coach who made me captain at Pennant Hills used to say, 'Focus on the game plan and the result will take care of itself'.

Epilogue

When Barnaby Howarth was young, he wanted to be an AFL superstar – he thought he had to be something 'exceptional' to be happy. However, after going without so many things after the stroke, he now sees that a good, honest life is more than enough to keep him happy. He has played a night final for the Swans on the MCG, and kicked goals on the SCG, but his greatest football memory is kicking a goal for Pennant Hills fourth grade at Ern Holmes oval in his 100th game; being admitted to the Sydney AFL Hall of Fame later that year showed him that he didn't need anything exceptional to be happy. As long as he can look himself in the mirror at the end of each day and say that he gave one hundred per cent to everything he did that day, he is a happy man.

As much as Barnaby is looking forward to continuing his motivational speaking career, what he's looking forward to more than anything else is just being a regular, decent Australian bloke. Paying his taxes, mowing the lawn and getting married are all things he nearly missed out on, so he doesn't want an exceptional life anymore, a normal one is more than enough. You don't need to be prime minister or the CEO of a big corporation to be happy or to be doing something worthwhile; just being an ordinary person is something to be proud of.

Post script:
Once a footballer,
always a footballer

After playing his one hundredth game of footy with the Pennant Hills Demons, Barnaby thought he was done with the sport as a player, so when plans were put in motion for an old boys game, he watched with interest, but with no intention of getting involved. As the team list started taking shape, however, he realised he had to play.

'Why? asked Denise. 'I thought you were done with all that now.'

'Well, yes, me, too, but…' It was hard to put into words; it was an itch, an impulse, a deep-seated need to get involved – he'd even coached the son of one of the members of the old boys team in the under eighteens!

'Does it feel right to do it?' Ross asked, getting to the heart of the matter.

'Yes, it does. I'll regret it if I pass up the chance to play.'

Ross grinned. 'So do it.'

Barnaby was soon prepared, he had all his gear, he was raring to go, and yet the day of the match inched closer with agonising slowness. Finally it arrived and the weather couldn't have been better; it was clear and sunny, bright, with the crisp bite of winter in the air, just perfect for players and spectators alike.

The team were almost all changed and ready but there was still one old boy missing.

'Where is he?' one of them asked.

'Must have got held up,' said Barnaby. 'He'll be here, though, he wouldn't miss this for the world.'

Just then their missing player crashed into the changing room. 'Sorry I'm late,' he said, and he set about getting changed as quickly as possible.

'Where've you been?' asked the coach. 'I thought we'd been stood up.'

'When I went to get my kit together, I realised I didn't have any boots; I threw them out a few years ago,' the latecomer said. He held up a bag from a sports shop and grinned sheepishly. 'I had to stop off and buy a pair.'

He fended off the good-natured heckling, then the coach called for order. After giving his usual pep talk, he finished up by saying, 'Now remember, lads, there are only two team rules for this match: no hand balling, and no thinking!'

Barnaby had reckoned he was as well prepared for the game as he could have been, but he was surprised by how physically demanding it all was. One of his team-mates copped a hip to the side of the head and another was laid out after he'd just kicked the ball.

'I don't remember it being this tough,' one of them said to Barnaby during a break in play. 'Must be getting old!'

'We're still winning, though,' said Barnaby.

His team mate laughed. 'Old but wily, eh?'

'Yeah, and then there're the umpiring decisions!'

The match got underway again and Hound Dog got the ball to Barnaby in an open goal square. He took the mark, played on and sealed the win for the Old Boys.

'Fantastic!' Hound Dog shouted as the team celebrated their victory.

Afterwards everyone headed off to the pub for a few beers and to trade stories old and new through the night. Sometimes it doesn't matter that you've heard a tale so many times you know what's coming; it's the company and the camaraderie and the atmosphere that makes it magical.

Nobody really cared who had won or lost, only that they had taken part.

Notes:

_____

_____

_____

_____

_____

_____

_____

_____

_____

_____

_____

_____

_____

_____

_____

_____

_____

_____

_____

_____

_____

Notes:

_____

_____

_____

_____

_____

_____

_____

_____

_____

_____

_____

_____

_____

_____

_____

_____

_____

_____

_____

_____

Connect with Barnaby

Website

http://barnabyhowarth.com.au/

Facebook

https://www.facebook.com/barnaby.howarth

Twitter

@barnabyhowarth

With special thanks to Julie Lewthwaite

The story of my ... story

When I finished writing my autobiography, I couldn't shake the feeling that I hadn't done my story justice, so I sought a professional writer, with a brief to tell my life story in an entertaining, fictional style, and UK-based writer Julie Lewthwaite answered the call.

I sent Julie everything I had that helped tell my story – I sent her my autobiography, news articles, documentaries, news videos and blogs, and I asked her to mould them into a single, entertaining book, and *Playing IN THE PUDDLES* is the result.

Who is Julie?

Julie Lewthwaite is a published author of both non-fiction and fiction, and a member of the Society of Authors. She also works as a freelance writer, ghostwriter, editor and proofreader.

Julie owns Miscandlon & Lewthwaite Writing Services with Steven Miscandlon. They can be contacted at:

enquiries@mlwritingservices.co.uk

Made in the USA
Charleston, SC
15 May 2015